# The Italian Invasion of Ethiopia

*A Captivating Guide to Mussolini's War
in Abyssinia*

# Free Bonus from Captivating History (Available for a Limited time)

Hi History Lovers!

Now you have a chance to join our exclusive history list so you can get your first history ebook for free as well as discounts and a potential to get more history books for free! Simply visit the link below to join.

Captivatinghistory.com/ebook

Also, make sure to follow us on Facebook, Twitter and Youtube by searching for Captivating History.

# Table of Contents

# Introduction – Ethiopia's Unbroken Chain of Civilization

Ethiopia is a place where myth and legend seem to come to life. Ethiopia is mentioned in the Bible and in Greek myths. It was a land of wonder then, and it remains a land of wonder today. Ethiopia is positioned on the Horn of Africa, where the Red Sea meets the sands of Arabia, which means it has always been at a crossroads. The Queen of Sheba was said to have shuttled back and forth between Ethiopia and Israel with ease, and one can only wonder about the storied history that unfolded along her path.

The very fact that Ethiopia has been around so long and has a culture and history that forges a largely uninterrupted chain of events is in itself a great testament to the people who inhabited the country. Very few parts of the world can claim to have an ongoing civilization with roots that date back tens of thousands of years.

For example, almost everyone is familiar with ancient Egypt and its pharaohs and pyramids. Ancient Egypt was a great civilization. But does anyone speak Egyptian today? No, they do not because it is a dead language. And ancient Egypt eventually succumbed to outside influences, with other civilizations superimposed upon its framework.

The ancient Ethiopian civilization was as old as Egypt. Yet unlike Egypt, which was repeatedly conquered by outside powers, including the Greeks, Romans, Arabs, Turks, and British, Ethiopia has stood strong and unconquered. Yes, Ethiopia's government looks different today than it did all those years ago, but it never had to bow to a foreign power.

At the time of the Italian invasion in the 1930s, Ethiopia was the only indigenous African land that had not been forcibly conquered. The word "indigenous" must be stressed here because some have cited Liberia as another possible contender for an African nation that has never been colonized. But Liberia is not an ancient independent nation in the same sense that Ethiopia is.

Liberia was actually founded by Americans in the 1820s as a potential home for freed slaves. Ethiopia's history is much different, as its history as a free and independent nation, indigenous to the African continent, dates back thousands of years.

And it is important to note that Ethiopia remains unconquered. Although the Italians invaded and occupied a few major cities for a few years, the struggle to expel them never ended. Ethiopian fighters remained in the bush, eking out survival on the outskirts until they could drive the Italian interlopers from their lands. The Ethiopians knew what was at stake, and they fought not as if their lives depended on it but as if their very civilization depended on it.

And they were right to do so because their civilization did depend on them. If the Italians had had their way and had successfully annexed Ethiopia as an Italian colony, the Ethiopian civilization would look completely different than it does today.

This book chronicles the Italian invasion of Ethiopia and the heroic resistance that ultimately pushed the invaders out.

# Chapter 1 – Adwa—The Invasion Before the Invasion

*"God, in his bounty, has struck down my enemies and enlarged my empire and preserved me to this day. I have reigned by the grace of God. As we must all die sometime, I will not be afflicted when I die. Enemies have come who would ruin our country. They have passed beyond the sea which God gave us as a frontier. With God's help I will get rid of them."*

*-Menelik II*

To understand the Italian invasion of Ethiopia in 1936, it is important to take a look at a previous invasion that had been foiled decades before. In 1896, Italian troops infamously rushed to battle in Ethiopia, seeking to forcibly coerce the Ethiopians into the Italian fold.

The Italians were latecomers to 19th-century colonialism. Even though Spain, France, Portugal, and the Netherlands had already forged sprawling colonies, Italy was slow to do so. The Italian Peninsula faced years of strife and disintegration. It did not become a fully unified nation until 1871.

The Italians were insecure about their position among the great powers of Europe, and they clearly felt as if they were playing a game of catch-up. The Scramble for Africa was in full force, and the Italians were absolutely desperate to get a slice of the African pie.

Even so, Italian heads of state would later come to claim that the knock-down, drag-out fight that resulted in Adwa stemmed from a simple misunderstanding. It was a misunderstanding over a treaty that had previously been signed between the Kingdom of Italy and the Empire of Ethiopia.

Prior to the breakout of hostilities, the Italians had sought to win concessions through niceties and diplomacy rather than warfare. They already controlled a small toehold in northern Ethiopia with their holdings in Eritrea. So, the Italians considered Ethiopia an important and powerful neighbor and wanted to deal with it.

Part of this diplomatic push was due to the fact that the Ethiopians had already beaten back a previous Italian incursion. Italians had attempted to make inroads into northern Ethiopia but were waylaid by Ethiopian forces led by Emperor Johannes IV near Dogali. Known as the Dogali massacre, it is said that as many as five hundred Italians were killed.

By the time of the Battle of Adwa, Ethiopia was ruled by a powerful Ethiopian monarch named Menelik II. Rather than push their luck with Menelik by using force, the Italians tried to diplomatically wrangle concessions from the Ethiopian ruler. The Italians convinced Menelik to sign the infamous Treaty of Wuchale.

This treaty had two different versions that said two different things. The version written in Italian basically had Menelik signing off on Ethiopia becoming a protectorate of Italy. The Amharic (Ethiopian) version said nothing of the sort. When Menelik learned that he had been diplomatically duped, he demanded a retraction.

Italian Foreign Minister Pietro Antonelli, who was at Menelik's court working as a direct link between Italy and Ethiopia, attempted to find some sort of compromise. At one point, it almost seemed as if a breakthrough had been made. Antonelli stressed over and over again the importance of Italy saving face and came up with an altered version of the treaty. While this treaty did not make Ethiopia a protectorate, it did give Italy a preferred status in Ethiopian affairs.

Menelik nearly went for the deal before his wife, Empress Taytu, suddenly intervened. Disgusted by Antonelli's attempts to "save face," she is said to have exclaimed, "We too must maintain our dignity! You want other countries to see Ethiopia as your protégé, but that will never be!"

Hitting a dead end, Antonelli and his fellow Italian diplomats left Ethiopia soon after. From this point forward, the clouds of war loomed larger than ever on the horizon. In October 1895, Italy made the first move. The Italians sent a large contingent of soldiers across the Mareb River, which served as a border between Italian and Ethiopian territory.

Menelik was watching and waiting in the meantime, and he immediately dispatched a force of some 100,000 Ethiopian soldiers to meet the Italian advance. In the northern Ethiopian region of Tigray, Menelik's troops engaged the Italians on December 7th, 1895.

And as this engagement was taking place, another batch of Ethiopian soldiers, under a commander by the name of Fitawrari Gebeyehu, stormed an Italian compound just over the borderlands between Italian territory and Ethiopian territory. Since the Italian base was situated on a hill, taking it was literally an uphill struggle.

Despite the hardship, the tenacious Ethiopian fighters were able to swarm in and shut down the Italians. About one thousand Italians were killed. Due to the Ethiopians' decisive victory, Fitawrari Gebeyehu became known as Commander "Gobez-eyehu." In the Ethiopian language (Amharic), the word *gobez* means "good." The fact that Fitawrari Gebeyehu was able to decisively defeat the Italians made him very good in the eyes of his troops.

Ethiopia's success continued to mount all the way up until that great showdown on March 1st, 1896: the Battle of Adwa. During this battle, the Italians were outnumbered, but their armaments were much better. The guns used by the Ethiopians were mostly outdated rifles, while the Italians had more modern artillery.

However, Ethiopia had one great boon on its side. Shortly before the war erupted, the Russians gifted the Ethiopians with around 135 artillery pieces. It remains to be seen how decisive this might have been in the long run, but the use of these weapons certainly provided some help to the Ethiopian war effort.

The Ethiopians smashed into three Italian columns of troops. Soon the Italians were utterly routed and on their heels. By the time the battle came to a close, the Italians were humiliated, as it was a disastrous defeat.

For the first time in history, a European power was soundly defeated by an African power. And the Italians would not take it very well. Resentment over this defeat would still be simmering when fascists took control of Italy in 1922. The leader of the Italian fascists, Benito Mussolini, kept his cards close to his chest and was initially quite friendly with Ethiopia.

Of course, this was merely a repeat of the same subterfuge of the past. By the early 1930s, Mussolini was presenting himself as the best friend of Ethiopian Emperor Hailie Selassie. Prior to the second Italian invasion, he invited Emperor Selassie to Rome, where he rolled out the red carpet for him.

But it would soon be realized that Mussolini was merely playing out of the same old playbooks of his predecessors. Just like Pietro Antonelli, he was simply seeking to wine and dine the Ethiopian emperor, luring him into a false sense of security right before dropping the hammer.

# Chapter 2 – Italian Intrigue and Subterfuge

*"The Duke of Aosta spoke with considerable optimism about the condition of the Ethiopian Empire. I must, however, add that among the many people who have come from there he is the only optimist. He urges [us] to avoid a conflict with France which would bring on to the high seas the task of pacifying our empire and would jeopardize the conquest itself."*

*-Ciano*

Haile Selassie was proclaimed emperor of Ethiopia on April 2nd, 1930. However, he had been the acting leader long before that, acting as administrator under the deceased Menelik II's daughter, Zewditu. After Zewditu passed, Selassie, who had long been the true power behind the throne, was officially proclaimed.

Zewditu was not considered a strong ruler. She also had no natural heirs. Her cousin, Selassie, then known as Tafari Mekonnen, had previously served as a regional ras or "governor." He became her prime minister, as well as a prime contender for the throne. Tafari was an able governor, and he and a powerful clique of nobles were the ones who primarily governed Ethiopia, although they did so in Zewditu's name.

Selassie, who would ultimately be the last in a long line of Ethiopian monarchs, had to fight tooth and nail for his crown. Multiple factions rose up against him in various regions of Ethiopia. The country was in turmoil for much of the 1920s. Selassie had to put out multiple fires as he rose to the task of ruling as emperor.

In Italy, a fascist coup took over the Italian government in 1922. This new Italian leadership was big on symbolism and sought to restore the prestige of Rome's ancient past, back when the Italian boot was the seat of the vast Roman Empire.

Mussolini initially kept his cards close to his chest. In 1924, when Selassie was still acting as regent for Zewditu, Mussolini invited Selassie to the Italian capital for a personal meeting. Mussolini was quite friendly with Selassie (then known as Ras Tafari), and the two discussed many future potential relations between the two nations. First and foremost on Selassie's mind was to secure a port to the Red Sea.

Benito Mussolini immediately seized upon this interest and offered up the port of Assab in Italian-controlled Eritrea. Mussolini promised to grant the Ethiopians control of the port for a period of ninety-nine years as long as Ethiopia granted Italy a favored nation status. This status would put Italy at the front of the line as it pertained to privileges, concessions, and immunities.

However, despite all of Mussolini's niceties, Selassie smelled a rat. He was certainly well versed enough in Ethiopian history to know that Prime Minister Mussolini's talk of granting Italy a favored nation status would lead the two countries down the same path that led to the Battle of Adwa.

The Italians had tricked the Ethiopians in the past with similarly vague and untrustworthy deals. As such, Selassie was quick to reject any such agreement. The Italians rubbed the Ethiopians the wrong way shortly after this meeting when they decided to construct railroad tracks that ran from Italian Eritrea in Ethiopia's north to Italian Somalia in Ethiopia's east.

Like a bunch of bad neighbors, who, out of nowhere, decide to construct a fence that runs right through someone else's yard, the Italians were overstepping their bounds with their actions. This was outrageous to Emperor Haile Selassie, but he suspected that the Italians were just daring him to do something about it. They wanted to provoke him and perhaps spark a war over the railroad.

Selassie very much believed in the necessity of international processes and organizations to diffuse conflicts. He had seen to it that Ethiopia joined the League of Nations, an international organization designed to keep the peace. So, rather than confronting the Italians directly, Selassie complained of this egregious trespass to the League of Nations.

His complaint to the League of Nations did the trick since the Italians had no rational explanation as to why they would do such a thing. All the Ethiopians had to do was point at the railroad track running through their land, and it was quite obvious to everyone else that the Italians were in the wrong. After wasting much energy, effort, and money, the Italians had once again been utterly humiliated. They were forced to back down, and they dismantled their railroad.

Italian officials were raging over this turn of events behind the scenes, and it would not be long before they sought to connect Italian Eritrea and Italian Somalia, this time not through a railroad but by annexing Ethiopia outright. They wanted to create a greater Italian East Africa. Haile Selassie, who was officially crowned emperor in 1930, had scarcely a few years on the throne behind him before he had to deal with an outright invasion by the Italian armed forces.

An image of Haile Selassie.
https://commons.wikimedia.org/wiki/File:Haile_Selassie_in_full_dress_(cropped).jpg

The first outbreak of this struggle emerged on December 5th, 1934, when shots were fired between Italian and Ethiopian troops in the border regions between Ethiopia and Italian Somalia. The reason behind the skirmish remains unclear, but it is known the Ethiopians suffered far more casualties in this exchange than the Italians.

Although it was unclear why the first shot rang out, it is obvious conflict would have arisen regardless because the Italians were encroaching upon Ethiopia's borders. This encroachment was most visibly demonstrated by the building of a fortress at the Walwal oasis, which straddled the Ethiopian border. This was the provocation that led to hostilities, but historians aren't sure if there was a simple misunderstanding that led to the first shot or if it was a planned attack. Regardless, Italian officials stomped their feet and raised their voices, demanding that Ethiopia be held solely accountable for the incident.

Haile Selassie was likely outraged as well, but he knew that Ethiopia needed some time to prepare for war. So, he sought to cool down the heat in the room and avoid a war he knew that his nation was not yet ready to fight. A few days later, on December 9th, he requested that Italy agree to negotiate the matter diplomatically. He cited the terms of a previous treaty between Ethiopia and Italy dating back to 1928 called the Treaty of Friendship, which outlined how to handle disputes.

The Italians did not want to be friends. They huffed and puffed and then began making absolutely absurd demands. For instance, they demanded an official apology from the emperor himself. Even more ridiculous, they demanded that a group of high-ranking Ethiopians appear at Walwal, near where the incident occurred, and salute the Italian flag. Mussolini and his cronies were basically trying to get the Ethiopians to grovel at their feet and beg for forgiveness. They also demanded the equivalent of around $100,000 in reparations.

It remains unclear who fired that first shot that day, but even if the Ethiopians had started it, the terms demanded by the Italians were absolutely untenable. Haile Selassie realized that direct negotiations with the Italian government were futile. He once again sought an international arbiter for the conflict. On December 14th, he presented the matter to the League of Nations. The League of Nations had weighed in on the railroad incident in the past and brought it to a peaceful conclusion. Haile Selassie hoped it could step in once again and bring peace.

Of course, the Italians had no desire to end the matter peaceably. Even after the League of Nations stepped in, the Italians refused to listen to reason.

Behind the scenes, much intrigue was afoot between the Italians and another League of Nations member, France. Initially, the French were fairly supportive of Ethiopia. They wanted to have a strong Ethiopian regime to maintain the status quo. But after a series of internal struggles erupted between the death of Menelik and the rise of Haile Selassie, the French became disenchanted and more sympathetic to Italy's ambitions in the region.

The French did not want Italy to invade Ethiopia, but they were ready to allow the Italians to have a stronger hand if war broke out. French Prime Minister Pierre Laval hinted as much in 1932 when Italian Foreign Minister Dino Grandi paid a visit. That same year, when Ethiopian Emperor Haile Selassie approached, seeking aid in the procurement of arms and the construction of infrastructure, the French remained tight-lipped and refused to get involved.

This French accommodation for and appeasement of Italian ambitions would eventually lead to the Laval-Mussolini Agreement, which was forged in January 1935. In this agreement, the Italians once again raised the idea of their ambitions in Ethiopia.

The Italian forces under Emilio de Bono launched a full-scale invasion on October 3$^{rd}$, 1935, by once again crossing the Mareb River in northern Ethiopia. The only thing that would have stopped the Italian invasion at this point would have been the direct intervention by a powerful League of Nations member. The most likely candidate for this would have been Great Britain.

Within the halls of power in Britain, the matter was discussed, but British intervention was viewed as a highly unfavorable decision. It wasn't that the British did not have sympathy for Ethiopia; many did. But many were also weary of war and sought to avoid British entanglement in regional problems. This spirit of appeasement was on full display when British Prime Minister Neville Chamberlain famously caved into Hitler's demands (with none other than Mussolini in attendance) in Munich in 1938.

After the Munich Agreement was signed, with Hitler receiving huge tracts of land, Chamberlain came home and falsely claimed that he had just won "peace for our time." As just about every historian will confirm, in reality, Neville Chamberlain's appeasement only laid the groundwork for World War Two. And in many ways, the British appeasement of Italian aggression in Ethiopia was a prelude to this same phenomenon.

In Britain's efforts to avoid conflict with the Italians, many in the top brass of the British military were rather fond of exaggerating the prowess of the Italian military. Reports came in that if Britain went to war with

Italy, her fleet would be decimated in the Italian-dominated Mediterranean. The ability of the Italian air force was also greatly exaggerated, with military planners insisting that Britain's anti-aircraft capabilities were not in good enough shape to fend off prolonged Italian bombardment. In consideration of the later Battle for Britain in 1940, when the British ably fended off a concerted assault conducted by the German air force, which was much more advanced and powerful than the Italian air force, such claims seem utterly absurd.

The British ultimately viewed the conflict between the Ethiopians and Italians as a regional conflict, and they sought to wash their hands of it to avoid a larger confrontation. However, their refusal to put out this small fire would help to lead to the terrible conflagration of a world war. Some British officials, such as Foreign Secretary Sir Samuel Hoare, made light of and even justified the Italian aggression as nothing more than empire building, something that was not too dissimilar to Britain's conquests in the past.

As Hoare put it at the height of Italian aggression in 1935, "I am bored by this Italian-Abyssinian dispute, and really I fail to see why we should interfere. Why should England fight Italy over Abyssinia, when most of our far flung Empire has been won by conquest?"

Interestingly, Samuel Hoare seemed to do a complete 180 by September of that same year when the invasion was already underway. Sir Samuel Hoare spoke before the League of Nations on September 11th, 1935, and seemed to come out on the side of intervention to save Ethiopia.

Attempting to speak for the League itself, he stated, "We believe that small nations are entitled to a life of their own and to such protection as can collectively be afforded to them in the maintenance of their national life. It is not enough to insist collectively that war shall not occur or that war, if it occurs, shall be brought to an end. Something must be done to remove the causes from which war is likely to arise." But as the British dithered and went back and forth with their convictions, the Italian invasion of Ethiopia continued forward in full force.

# Chapter 3 - The Invasion Gets Underway

*"It is humiliating to remain with our hands folded while others write history. It matters little who wins. To make a people great it is necessary to send them to battle even if you have to kick them in the pants. That is what I shall do."*

*-Benito Mussolini*

At the outset of Italy's invasion of Ethiopia, ironically enough, the very first town the Italians pummeled was Adwa. This, of course, could not have been an accident. The Italians still smarted from their previous defeat, so they were sure to knock out Adwa first.

Mussolini ensured the Italians were armed to the teeth and that their numbers were numerically strong. He was not willing to leave anything to chance. When ruminating on these things, Mussolini was once heard to remark, "For the lack of a few thousand men we lost the day at Adwa! We shall never make that mistake. I am willing to commit a sin of excess but never of deficiency."

Yes, the memory of the previous Italian defeat at the Battle of Adwa was still quite strong. Even before the Italians left Eritrea, as they passed through the Eritrean town of Asmara, they could not help but see the colossal monument of an Italian soldier pointing southward to Ethiopia. On the statue, which was built in commemoration of the Italians who had died at Adwa, these words were inscribed: "Italians, remember we died for our country, and one day will cancel this defeat by victory."

The words were supposed to instill the idea that the Italians would one day avenge this past wrong. Never mind the fact that the Italians were wrong in the first place and never should have started trouble with the Ethiopians in the beginning. But as was common with fascist propaganda, the truth could often be stretched beyond all recognition to meet the ends of what the state wants.

At any rate, on October 6th, de Bono and his men collided with Ethiopian troops in the vicinity of Adwa. The Ethiopian forces were led by Ethiopian commander Ras Seyoum Mengesha.

Now, before we go any further, it must be understood that the term "Ras" is the Ethiopian term for "governor." Many of the regional warlords who operated under the aegis of the Ethiopian emperor are referred to as "Ras." Haile Selassie himself was previously known as Ras Tafari. His birth name is Tafari, and he was recognized as the regional governor of Harar.

As an interesting aside, it is worth noting that the Rastafarian movement that sprang up in Jamaica stems from Emperor Haile Selassie. Prior to Ras Tafari becoming emperor, he was idolized by Jamaican philosopher Marcus Garvey. Due to Garvey's high praise, many Jamaicans became intrigued by this powerful Ethiopian known as Ras Tafari. They created a quasi-religious movement centered around him, which would be dubbed Rastafarianism.

In later years, the Rastas would even go as far as to say that Haile Selassie was some sort of god. Haile Selassie was quite perplexed and perhaps a little embarrassed by all of this. Selassie was a strong and devout Christian and repeatedly told the Rastas that he was just a man and that the only one who deserved worship was Jesus Christ. Yet the strange devotion to Selassie persisted, and it even persists to this day.

It just goes to show you how easily some religions can get started. It might sound absurd to us today to start a religion around a governor. Just think of Californians today starting a religion around Governor Gavin Newsom; we could dub it "GovGavinianism." It sounds utterly bizarre, but that is precisely what the Rastafarians did with Ras Tafari.

Before we get too off track here talking about Rastas and Rastafarianism, let us get back to the main topic of conversation: the Italian invasion of Ethiopia. At the outset of the invasion, the Ethiopians were ready for a hard fight, and regional chiefs, such as the aforementioned Ras Seyoum Mengesha, rallied their troops and were ready to lead. However, the Italians were prepared to fight dirty.

As the Ethiopians attempted to engage Italian forces on the ground, Italian airpower swarmed overhead and used the Ethiopian troops as target practice. This was exactly what Haile Selassie had feared and was trying to avoid. In the turmoil of the 1920s, when multiple rounds of civil conflicts within Ethiopia largely prevented the modernization of arms, Italy built up its professional army and developed an air force. Ethiopia did not have much in the way of air defenses.

It would be wrong to say that Ethiopia had no air defenses, though. Ethiopia had a few planes, and it also had a handful of anti-aircraft guns, the latter of which were able to successfully take out a total of eight Italian planes during the war. But this fledgling start of Ethiopian aerial power was certainly no match for the fully developed Italian air force. For the most part, the only real defense that Ethiopian troops on the ground had against the Italian flying menace was to dive into a ditch for cover.

Haile Selassie, who had just recently secured his grip on power, needed more time to modernize the Ethiopian armed forces. But time had run out. Completely overwhelmed, Ras Seyoum Mengesha's forces were compelled to surrender. The Ethiopian fighters stationed in the nearby city of Mek'ele in the region of Tigray did not even bother resisting.

The Tigrayans, who had long felt themselves on the periphery of Ethiopian society anyway, decided to throw in their lot with the invaders and fight alongside the Italians. This defection was led by the governor of the eastern Tigray region, Haile Gugsa.

Mek'ele was as far as Emilio de Bono would go. In December, he was relieved of his command since things were not progressing as quickly as Mussolini had planned.

Although things were not going as planned, the Italians' aggression was nothing to write off. Still, it is important to remember that facts are often obscured by parties of the conflict in just about any instance of warfare.

For example, during the seizure of Adwa, some early press reports claimed that an Ethiopian hospital was bombed by the Italians. This was easily refuted when it was realized that there was no hospital in Adwa. Later in the war, the Italians accidentally dropped aerial bombardment on a Swedish Red Cross hospital, an event that actually did happen.

However, it is possible that later accounts of the Italians bombing an Ethiopian hospital in Adwa could be a conflation of events. The bombing of the Swedish Red Cross hospital could have been mixed up with the initial claims of the Italians bombing a nonexistent hospital in Adwa.

Unlike the imagined hospital in Adwa, the bombing of the Swedish Red Cross hospital was a real event and could have had some real consequences. The Swedes were certainly not happy with what the Italians were doing, that is for sure.

The Italians had a trend of harassing members of the Red Cross, the worst of which would occur in the spring of 1936 when a couple of Red Cross employees from Poland were taken as prisoners of war. First of all, humanitarian aid workers should have been considered non-combatants and entirely neutral to the conflict. But what was worse than them being captured in the first place was how they were treated.

They were interrogated and beaten. When it was found that one of them, Dr. Maksymiljian Stanislaw Belau, was actually a regional head for a field hospital, he was forced to issue a statement under duress. The statement declared that all previous claims of Italian mistreatment of the Red Cross were false. The idea that one could be bullied into denying previous instances of abuse is appalling.

At any rate, it is typically in the best interest of a country to make the other side look worse in a conflict. As it pertained to the aggression of the Italians, the actual tactics they employed were brutal enough, yet we find there are times when their atrocities were at least slightly embellished.

In the meantime, the League of Nations was finally prompted to take more action. As much as the League of Nations has been ridiculed as being highly ineffective, in reality, the League did serve its purpose. As ineffectual as the League might seem on the surface, it still served as an international forum and would at least start the process of holding other nations accountable for their actions. Without the League of Nations, there would have been no venue to address any concerns.

Although many would say it was too little too late, the League of Nations did (slowly) move into action after the Italians began their invasion. On October 19th, 1935, the League of Nations hit Italy with sanctions. Sanctions are a readily recognizable punishment on the world stage today, and they are largely carried out by the descendant and successor of the antiquated League of Nations: the United Nations.

Back then, as now, the whole purpose of sanctions was to cause a deliberate impact on the aggressor nation and stifle its tendency to use aggression. The sanctions on Italy were voted on at Geneva by almost all of the fifty-four member states assembled. These sanctions were aimed at crippling the Italian economy in the hopes that it would be enough to cause Mussolini to rethink his plans of blatant conquest. But Mussolini was not willing to turn back; instead, he was insistent that the Italian thrust should charge forward.

Of all the international players at this time, it could be said that Germany's position was the most paradoxical of all. Germany and Italy were not yet formally allied, and even though Adolf Hitler held some affinity for Benito Mussolini and Italian fascism, Mussolini's Italy had served as a roadblock to German ambitions in Austria. Germany was already readying itself for the annexation of Austria, but Italy had voiced its reservations.

For that reason, a defeat of Italy in Ethiopia was considered beneficial for German aims in Austria. Yet, at the same time, if Italy was victorious, the Germans believed that France and Britain would be weakened, opening the door for German aggression in western Europe. Hitler saw benefits in both outcomes. As a result, he attempted to play both sides of the fence at the outset of the Second Italo-Ethiopian War.

Although Germany was not actively involved with the sanctions against Italy, it and other nations pulled much of its economic support for Italy by curtailing trade with the aggressive nation. It is not talked about much, but Germany also gave some wartime aid to Ethiopia. Germany quietly sent ammunition and arms to the Ethiopians on the very eve of the conflict and during the initial stages of the war.

Germany was playing coy with the Italian situation. More than anything else, it feared backing Italy in case the Italians were served another humiliating defeat. Therefore, the Germans took a "wait and see approach." Germany's approach at this critical juncture is eerily similar to what many modern-day analysts believe China's approach is to the Russo-Ukraine War, which started in the early 2020s.

In recent years, China has attempted to present itself as a steadfast ally of Russia, yet ever since the Russians launched their invasion of Ukraine in 2021, the Chinese have taken a hands-off approach. And as the Russian war efforts took a turn for the worse, the Chinese have seemingly sought to distance themselves even further. Pragmatic China, just like Germany before, seems to be unwilling to voice its support for a potential loser in a major conflict.

Before taking any major action, the German high command wished to sit back and observe how this whole thing might play out. They did quietly render some aid to Ethiopia, including arms, ammunition, and even a few aircraft. It certainly was not enough to turn the tide, but if Italy were defeated, such an unexpected kindness likely would have been remembered. As terrible as he was, Hitler, ever the plotting mastermind, wished to cover all of his bases and prepare for just about any eventuality.

Despite heavy losses suffered by Ethiopia, there were a few victorious moments for the Ethiopian armed forces. As the northern Ethiopian front collapsed, the Ethiopians on the eastern and western fronts continued to struggle valiantly against the invaders. The western troops were led by Emperor Selassie's commander, Ras Imru (sometimes spelled Emeru). Ras Imru managed to eke out a stunning success on December 15th, 1935, when his troops waylaid a group of Askaris, Eritrean soldiers who were loyal to the Italians. The Askaris were led by Italian commander Major Luigi Griniti.

Major Griniti was attempting to lead the Askaris through the strategic pass of Dambagwina when Ras Imru's troops caught them by surprise. The most stunning incident during this battle was when Imru's forces were able to draw several Italian tanks into a devastating trap. The Ethiopians lured the tanks into the narrow reaches of the pass on rough terrain, which made maneuvering the tanks very difficult.

Ethiopian warriors proceeded to push boulders behind and in front of the column of tanks, effectively trapping them in place. Ethiopian fighters then bravely stormed the tanks, and with hand grenades and, in some instances, even their bare hands, they completely disabled them. The quick-thinking Ethiopians realized that one hand grenade tossed down the radiator of a tank was enough to put it out of commission for good. If that did not work, they destroyed the treads of the tank so it could no longer move.

Once the tanks were out of commission, the terrified Italian occupants were pulled from the tanks and either killed on the spot or taken as prisoners of war. Much of Imru's success was due to his ability to quickly strike against the enemy and then just as rapidly retreat. With his finely honed fighting instinct, he knew when to strike and when to evacuate, and he was quite successful at both.

No matter how hard the Italians tried, they could not corner the Ethiopian troops. At one point, Imru successfully led a fully intact brigade of ten thousand Ethiopian fighters across the Takkaze River, safely out of reach of the Italians. Actions like these left the Italian conquest inconclusive even after the Italians captured the country's capital. Just like Napoleon, who occupied Moscow but was unable to defeat the Russian army, Mussolini was facing a problem. The Ethiopian forces continued to resist and carry on the fight.

In the east, Ethiopian troops were putting up some of the stiffest resistance to the Italians who poured in from Italian Somaliland (now part of the nation of Somalia). These fierce fighters dug huge trenches, which they could dive into when overhead Italian planes appeared. They were then able to bounce back up just in time to riddle approaching Italian soldiers with bullets. But as valiant and vigorous as the Ethiopian resistance was, the Italians, under the leadership of Italian General Rodolfo Graziani, relentlessly pushed westward.

In the first phase of the invasion, in the fall of 1935, the biggest thorn in Graziani's side was Ethiopian commander Ras Desta, who ran the show in Sidamo Province. Desta had a huge army at his disposal, said to be about eighty thousand strong. Initially, Desta's force restrained Graziani, preventing his progress. If Rodolfo Graziani wanted to march on the Ethiopian capital, he had to get through Desta's troops first.

This was a formidable roadblock and could have caused Graziani a great setback in his ambitions. But even though Ras Desta was a brilliant commander, he made a mistake. Desta decided he wanted to take the initiative. Instead of merely restraining the Italians, he went on the offensive and launched an assault on Italian Somaliland. This attempted offensive did not go well. Once Desta's troops were out in the open, Graziani was able to attack them with Italian warplanes.

Bombs were dropped on the Ethiopian forces, and their supply lines buckled and broke. Desta's troops were soon starving. As the weeks progressed, the weakened Ethiopian troops became sick and died of various diseases. Due to all of these factors, the once-mighty army of Ras Desta was rapidly whittled down to a small fraction of what it once was. With Desta's forces shattered, the Italians under Rodolfo Graziani were able to continue their drive west toward the Ethiopian capital of Addis

Ababa.

In many ways, one of the biggest challenges the Italians faced during their march to the Ethiopian capital was logistics. Although the Italians had been widely praised for their capacity for road building (just consider the Apian Way! and had built up grand infrastructure in their colonies of Eritrea and Italian Somaliland, their roads ended as soon as they reached Ethiopian territory.

Yes, the Italian colonial roads often dead-ended into nothing more than mud and dirt. And Ethiopia itself had not yet built up its roadways. It was exceedingly difficult to move heavy equipment and vehicles across this terrain. So, even though the many military failures of the Italian military have been widely cited for their loss in the war, the fact that the Italians were as successful as they were in moving their forces through this rough terrain does say something about their keen sense of logistical maneuvering.

Nevertheless, as the Italian forces closed in on Addis Ababa, a last-ditch effort was planned to stave off complete defeat. The Ethiopians launched a counteroffensive in January 1936, where the vast bulk of what was left of the Ethiopian forces hurled themselves at the Italian army at the Battle of Tembien. The battle took place in a narrow mountain pass. The Ethiopians were able to swoop down on the Italians from all sides. They put up such a fierce fight that the Italians were nearly repelled.

A look at Italian artillery in the Battle of Tembien.
https://commons.wikimedia.org/wiki/File:AO-Etiopia-1936-A-artiglieria-nel-Tembien.jpg

Thousands of Ethiopian warriors surged into the Italian positions. Not all of the Ethiopians were equipped with guns; in fact, some were unarmed. But it did not matter. The Ethiopians rushed the Italians and ripped their machine guns right out of their hands. Many Ethiopians perished in the hail of bullets, but no matter how many perished, the Ethiopians just kept coming.

The Italians and their Eritrean allies were forced to give ground, and as they did so, they abandoned valuable weapons. The Ethiopians picked these up and began using them on the Italians, making their victory seem even more likely. This daring charge could have been a repeat of the Battle of Adwa in the First Italo-Ethiopian War. But unfortunately for the Ethiopians, Italian airpower once again ensured that an Ethiopian victory would not be possible.

As the Italian ground troops sustained major losses, the Italian planes roared overhead and began dropping incendiary bombs and poison shells of mustard gas. The Italians had established large chemical weapons facilities in the Eritrean city of Asmara, as well as in Mogadishu, the capital of Italian Somalia. And not so coincidentally enough, just before the war, a large number of chemical weapons had been produced and stockpiled.

The poison gas was not something the Ethiopians could escape. Even if they managed to duck down into improvised ditches to avoid explosive blasts, the mustard gas covered the battlefield. And as the Ethiopian defenders' lungs burned with fire and as they gasped for breath, the Ethiopian counteroffensive crumbled.

Even so, the struggle continued. The next major battle of note occurred south of Addis Ababa, the Battle of Ganale Doria, on January 12th, 1936. The Ethiopians fought hard, but the brutal butcher Rodolfo Graziani annihilated hundreds of Ethiopian troops. But to Graziani's great dismay, hundreds of his Eritrean Askari fighters defected to the Ethiopian side. The main bulk of the Ethiopian army regrouped, and on March 31st, 1936, Haile Selassie himself led what remained of the Ethiopian armed forces in the Battle of Maychew.

This pitched battle lasted for several hours, and once again, the Ethiopians threw everything they had against the Italians. The Ethiopian forces were divided into three army groups consisting of a few thousand troops. There was a group of crack soldiers present in the form of Selassie's Imperial Guard. These troops were tasked with the protection of Emperor Selassie. They were the best trained and had the best weaponry of all of the Ethiopian soldiers.

The Imperial Guard was armed with machine guns that were roughly on par with the arms of the Italians. These troops were virtually the only Ethiopian force that was on somewhat equal footing with Italian troops in battle. Some in Selassie's inner circle argued against this move, thinking that sending the Imperial Guard was an extravagant waste. It was argued that it would be more prudent to pull back in a ringed defense of the capital and make the Italians come to them.

Such a tactic does make sense since it would have forced the Italians to stretch their supply lines much thinner. If the Ethiopians played on their home field, as it were, they would have more advantages. The troops could have forced the Italians into a bloody urban battle, with deadly fighting in the streets of Addis Ababa. Tanks would not be effective in the narrow thoroughfares of Addis Ababa, and the air force would not be of much use either since the Italians would be grappling with Ethiopian fighters in the tight quarters of the capital.

Yes, in many ways, this might have been the best strategy. Interestingly enough, many on the emperor's war council refused to engage in such tactics. They believed it would be better to boldly march out with a large army and gallantly meet their foes in open combat than to hide in the city. The outdated medieval mindset of many of Selassie's commanders might have cost the Ethiopian army a last-minute victory.

At any rate, once this final group of Ethiopian warriors surged toward the enemy, Selassie directed these fearsome fighters to focus their fire on the Italian auxiliary Eritrean troops, which made up a large portion of the Italian force. The Imperial Guard was wildly successful at this feat, nearly wiping them out entirely. Yet, right when the Imperial Guard seemed to be on the verge of turning the tide, the Italians called in their fighter planes.

A vicious mixture of aerial bombardment from above and relentless Italian artillery below forced the Imperial Guard back. Often enough, the only defense against the Italian planes was the weather itself. If the weather was particularly rainy, windy, and cloudy, the battlefield might be obscured just enough to prevent the Italian pilots from doing much damage.

But when the clouds parted, the pilots could clearly see Ethiopian troop positions and supply lines below. And the Italian craft did not hesitate to shower them with bombs. Seeing that no further headway could be made under this onslaught, Emperor Haile Selassie was forced to order a tactical withdrawal. Even so, the Italians suffered heavy losses, and their advance toward the capital was significantly delayed.

If the Italians thought that taking Ethiopia would be a walk in the park, the more sober-minded among them must have realized this was not going to be the case. It is true that the Ethiopian losses were generally higher than the Italian losses, but the Italian death toll was still staggering. These Italian losses quickly led to a loss in morale among Italian troops, especially since the Italians—other than being outright conquerors—did not have any logical reason to be invading Ethiopia in the first place.

Despite the Ethiopians' heavy losses, they knew they were serving a just cause: the defense of their civilization against those who sought to topple it. As such, the reason and inspiration for continuing the fight were naturally stronger among the Ethiopians than it ever was for the Italians. The Ethiopians struggled on because they felt their national identity was at stake. The Italian soldiers fought and bled because the Italian high command told them to.

The gravest threat the Italian army faced was losing the will to continue fighting. If Italian troops became discouraged enough, the whole Italian operation would disintegrate due to their own dissatisfaction. It was always a challenge to keep the average Italian soldier's spirits up during the invasion.

One thing the Italians had going for them was the fact they were able to easily intercept the radio transmissions of Haile Selassie and his commanders. These intercepted messages kept the Italians up to date on troop positions and the generally dire straits of the Ethiopian army. The Italians could take these intercepted reports and use them as propaganda to encourage their own troops.

The Italian commanders would point to these reports as evidence that victory was almost theirs and encouraged the weary Italian soldiers to push on. One can only imagine an Italian commander pointing to these messages and confidently extolling his troops, "Look! The Ethiopians are being destroyed! Be encouraged, comrades! Victory is almost ours!"

But despite what these commanders told their men, the Ethiopians had a lot more fight in them.

# Chapter 4 - Italians Reach Addis and Haile Selassie Departs

*"A fanatic is one who can't change his mind and won't change the subject."*

*-Winston Churchill*

Despite the Italians' determination to drive straight to the Ethiopian capital in what is called the "March of the Iron Will," they did not reach Addis Ababa until May 5th, 1936. Even after the disaster of Maychew, there was still some fighting in northern Ethiopia around the former Ethiopian capital of Gondar.

Before Addis Ababa had been established, the ancient city of Gondar—an enchanting place steeped in history and even outfitted with medieval-style castles that still stand today—once served as the center of the Ethiopian world. The Italians seized Gondar on April 1st, and over the next few weeks, they solidified their grip on the surrounding region of Lake Tana.

Simultaneous to the Ethiopian resistance to Italian General Pietro Badoglio's march south, there was also continued fighting between what was left of the eastern Ethiopian army group and Italian General Rodolfo Graziani's troops, which had poured out of Italian Somalia.

An image of Pietro Badoglio.
https://commons.wikimedia.org/wiki/File:Pietro_Badoglio_3.jpg

Yes, there was still some resistance as the Italians closed in, but it amounted to little more than a speed bump. Even so, because of the great sacrifice of so many Ethiopian warriors, Haile Selassie had some precious time to figure out his next move. He and his subordinates agreed that the only thing left to be done was to have the emperor evacuate the country so that the Ethiopian leadership would survive even after the Italian occupation had run its course.

This decision was not made unilaterally by Haile Selassie. Instead, the imperial council voted, with twenty-one members voting for his exit and three voting for him to remain. Among the notables at the imperial council was Ras Kasa, who had struggled so hard against Italian forces in the previous months. Kasa was one of the most vocal proponents for the emperor going into exile.

Ras Kasa knew firsthand how hopeless the situation was. He realized that the Italians were not the only threats. Hostile factions in the Ethiopian countryside also posed a considerable risk, and the emperor no doubt presented an enticing target. Tribal groups in the countryside could range from indifferent to downright predatory. Kasa experienced this when Gala tribal warriors ambushed his army as they were being forced to retreat from the Italian advance.

Ethiopian scholar and historian Bahru Zewde has rightfully noted that this was the first instance in history that an Ethiopian emperor had the option to escape and lead from exile. In the past, when Ethiopia was much more isolated with very few contacts with the outside world, such a thing was not even possible. For example, back in the 1500s, Emperor Dawit II faced an invasion from an Islamic army hellbent on forcibly converting Christian Ethiopia into an Islamic state. Dawit had no choice but to fight until the bitter end. Ethiopia was ultimately saved due to the last-minute intervention of the Portuguese, but not before Emperor Dawit perished on the battlefield.

The fact that Haile Selassie did not meet a similar fate fighting the Italians led to some criticism, but in reality, leaving was the best thing for him to do, considering the circumstances at the time. Haile Selassie was an adept politician with strong international ties. His powerful links to the outside world and international institutions were his own personal trump card, and he was willing to play it. Nevertheless, it was with a sad and deeply troubled heart that Emperor Haile Selassie left his Ethiopian homeland behind.

After bidding those of his inner circle who remained goodbye, Haile Selassie took a train to the port of Djibouti. From there, he hopped on a British ship. Interestingly enough, just prior to his departure, it is said that General Graziani was tipped off that Selassie was on a train headed for Djibouti. He suggested to Mussolini that the train should be bombed to prevent Selassie from leaving the country. However, Mussolini supposedly ordered General Graziani to stay his hand, allowing Selassie to depart in peace.

Many reasons have been given for Mussolini's actions. Some have suggested that perhaps he wanted Selassie alive for continued negotiations, while others have pointed out that the Italians could not have been entirely certain which train Selassie was on and risked killing innocent civilians. Such an outrage would have further bloodied Italy's image in the press.

Still, others muse that Mussolini had a soft spot for Selassie as a person and did not want to kill him. He had previously engaged with the Ethiopian emperor on friendly terms; one can only wonder if the friendliness was not entirely put on after all. Even the most despotic of human beings can be surprisingly complex, so perhaps we will never really know. However, these surprising complexities are what make the twists and turns of history so intriguing.

There is perhaps a simpler explanation as to why Mussolini might have practiced restraint. He was still indebted to the French due to previous negotiations in the Laval-Mussolini Agreement, which allowed Italy to have a free hand in the region. No matter how much the Italians might have wanted to bomb Haile Selassie, it must be remembered that the Djibouti railroad was still French property. Blowing it up would not have endeared Mussolini to the French.

At any rate, Selassie's train made it to the port city of Djibouti without any hindrance, and he boarded a British ship called the *Enterprise*. He took it up through the Red Sea to Haifa in what was then the British-controlled mandate of Palestine. Here, a sad and dejected Selassie sought inspiration and guidance. He initially tried to find it by tapping into his deep religious faith.

The backdrop of Israel/Palestine was, therefore, quite fitting, and soon Selassie was traveling from Haifa to Jerusalem. This city was important not only because of Selassie's Christian faith but also because Haile Selassie was a part of the Solomonic dynasty, which claimed to be descended from the union of King Solomon and the Queen of Sheba. This union took place after the Ethiopian queen visited Jerusalem and supposedly developed a relationship with King Solomon. Their offspring, Menelik I (not to be confused with the later Menelik II), supposedly marks the beginning of imperial Ethiopia.

After a brief stay at the King David Hotel, Haile Selassie was granted asylum in England. But Haile Selassie was not going to just sit on his laurels. Once he had been ferried to Britain and arranged his accommodations there, he made his way to the seat of the League of Nations: Geneva, Switzerland.

Here, he ascended the stage and spoke before all assembled about the horrors the Italians had unleashed upon his country. Selassie's main aim was to galvanize the world to act and forcibly intervene to stop the Italians. Another lesser but also quite important goal was to prevent an end to the sanctions that had already been issued against Italy. The sanctions may have been halfhearted, but they were taking their toll on the Italian economy. The Italians were lobbying to have them removed now that they had "restored the peace."

During the session, just before Selassie rose to speak, a letter from Mussolini was read before the assembly that stated the Italian dictator's assertion that the "war was over" and that the Italians were committed to ensuring a peaceful status quo in the region. This was meant to be a reassurance to League members like Britain and France, whose number one concern was the prevention of a disruption in their own colonies.

Ironically enough, after this statement from Italian Prime Minister Benito Mussolini was read, Haile Selassie appeared behind the podium to speak. When Italian journalists saw Selassie, they began to hoot and holler, creating a terrible disturbance. They even flicked a nearby light switch on and off to cause a distraction.

The Romanian representative, Nicolae Titulescu, was bold enough to finally speak up. He demanded that the disruptive Italians be thrown out. His wish was granted, and Selassie was able to finish his address without disruption. It might have seemed like a minor act at the time, but Ethiopians would long remember Nicolae Titulescu as the one strong voice in Geneva that day. In their eyes, he was the person who stood up to tyranny. Nicole Titulescu stood up for Haile Selassie and essentially stood up for all Ethiopians.

Although Titulescu would perish in 1941, Selassie would still fondly recall that moment many years later, stating that Titulescu's noble actions have been "written in the hearts of all Ethiopians, and the memory of his deeds will live forever." Considering the fact that his image was placed among the saints at the shrine of the Holy Trinity Cathedral in the Ethiopian capital of Addis Ababa, the name of Nicolae Titulescu will indeed live on.

Once Haile Selassie's tormentors were silenced, he was able to speak at length about what had happened to his country. He highlighted the atrocities that had occurred and stressed the clear violations of international laws and even international norms that had been committed. He then reminded the League of its commitments to collective security and demanded it live up to its charter by standing up to Italy's aggression.

His pleas were largely ignored, but his ominous warning to the world that if they did not do something to stop this outrage, they would be next would become downright prophetic. Looking out at the crowd assembled at this League of Nations gathering, Haile Selassie stated, "It is us today. It will be you tomorrow." Haile Selassie's prediction would be seemingly fulfilled when Italy, Germany, and Japan unleashed aggression on much of the world, triggering World War Two.

# Chapter 5 – The Italian Occupation Begins

*"Abyssinia gave me its peculiar trials, as well as the normal ones. Most of the war was fought on the plateau at heights of 6,000 to 11,000 feet. So near the equator, the rarity of the atmosphere is so intensified that in terms of strain on the heart, lungs, and nerves, the effect was comparable to that of an altitude of 10,000 to 15,000 feet in the temperate zone. The difference between midday and midnight was often as much as 70 degrees. In Dankalia and on the seacoast I was to encounter temperatures as high as 140 in the shade; it was so hot that one gasped for breath, but I never minded heat very much. The intense cold of the nights on the plateau was much more bothersome to me. So was the dust. One hears much about the role of mud in wars, but the other extreme of dust is equally common and very distressing in its way. The campaign in Abyssinia was fought in a constant cloud of dust which choked and blinded one and covered clothes in layers. One has to live through wars to discover what an astonishing amount of punishment the human body can take. I often wondered how lungs could stand up under the quantities of dust that have to be swallowed."*

-Herbert Mathews, American correspondent on the ground in Ethiopia

It has been said that the first week of the Italian occupation was the worst. Just after the departure of Emperor Haile Selassie and right before the entrance of the Italians into the Ethiopian capital of Addis

Ababa, all hell broke loose. Any sense of the rule of law and standard procedure as it pertained to the lives of average, everyday Ethiopians evaporated into thin air, and violence became commonplace. However, the violence was not just at the hands of the Italians but from the Ethiopians themselves.

As the Ethiopian government was dismantled, it was as if a cork holding in hostility had been removed. Absolute mayhem broke out. Some have since suggested that perhaps covert agents working on the last orders of Haile Selassie were instigating the chaos to make the Italian seizure of the capital more chaotic and difficult. But there has been no proof that this was the case.

The rioting and looting that occurred were widespread and had an element of class warfare, as the poorer Ethiopians struck out against the rich Ethiopians. Very quickly, the whole city was a cauldron of simmering chaos. Ethiopian scholar Bahru Zewde described it as a kind of madness that took hold of the average person, which led to "a total breakdown of law and order."

Bolstering the theory that Selassie had somehow engineered this debacle, there was a persistent rumor afoot that just prior to Haile Selassie's departure, he personally sanctioned some of the lootings. He supposedly issued an announcement that the palace would be left unlocked and that the public was welcome to come and take whatever they wanted. Again, there is no proof that any such declaration was ever made, but the rumor persisted and seemed to encourage some of the looting that took place.

The situation was so bad that some came to welcome the arrival of the Italians. After all, the Italians were sure to be able to strongarm some sense of stability out of the chaos that had erupted by way of sheer brute force. There are those who have wondered if this was a part of the Italian plan to begin with. The Italians seemed to slightly delay securing the capital just long enough to allow all of this terrible looting and rioting to play out. When they entered the city on May 5th, 1936, they almost appeared as peacemakers.

Italian troops advancing on Addis Ababa.
https://en.wikipedia.org/wiki/File:AO-Etiopia-1936-H-Cavalleria-indigena-verso-Addis-Abeba.jpg

Due to the unrest, many likely breathed a sigh of relief when General Pietro Badoglio led his troops into the city and used the threat of their mighty firepower to demand the rioters cease and desist. The Italian guns were very convincing. And if that were not enough, the Italians soon made the act of looting a capital offense punishable by the death penalty. This rule was enforced as soon as it was on the books, with an estimated one hundred or so Ethiopians being executed during the first week of the Italian administration.

Pietro Badoglio's successor, Rodolfo Graziani, would later build on the harshness of this decree by not only executing looters but also anyone who was deemed to be subversive to Italian governance. This broadness of the law gave the green light for trigger-happy and fearful Italian officials to apprehend and execute anyone who they deemed suspicious. As one can imagine, this only made an already toxic situation even worse.

An image of Rodolfo Graziani.

In the climate of fear and paranoia that developed, even those Ethiopians who sincerely wished to cooperate with the Italians ran the risk of somehow having their actions misconstrued at the slightest provocation. In one infamous incident, the bishop of the town of Dessie, which is situated on the road north of Addis Ababa, was executed because members of his community had launched attacks on the capital. It was claimed that he had been an advisor of the militant group, but there is no proof that this was the case. It seems more likely that he was targeted because he was a high-profile figure from Dessie, and the Italians wanted to shock and frighten the entire town with his public execution.

Italian General Rodolfo Graziani would later justify such actions, citing spiritual leaders, such as the bishop, as being the greatest threat to Italian hegemony. Graziani believed the spiritual leaders of Ethiopia had the ears of the populace and were the most likely to stir up an uprising. As Rodolfo Graziani himself later put it, "I learned through departmental channels and police headquarters that the greatest menace to public order came from the soothsayers, traditional story tellers. It was essential to root out this unhealthy and dangerous element [so] I gave orders that all the soothsayers, story tellers, and witch doctors were to be rounded up and shot." Along with the bishop of Dessie's death, Graziani also oversaw the execution of Archbishop Peter of Addis Ababa.

Ethiopia was a land steeped in Orthodox Christianity, and to have their religious leaders viewed as nothing more than "soothsayers, story tellers, and witch doctors" is certainly distressing. In reality, Ethiopia's Christian roots run just about as deep as Rome's.

Nevertheless, the Italians, most of whom were (at least) nominally Catholic, could have cared less whether the Ethiopians were fellow Christians or not. In fact, they sought to befriend the Muslims of Ethiopia as a means of dividing and conquering. They figured the Muslims had been suppressed by Christian Ethiopians for a long time and would become willing allies in their quest to suppress the traditional Ethiopian culture and society.

At any rate, at the outset of the Italians' entry into the capital, the rioting and outward manifestations of disturbance soon calmed down. Well, enough at least for Pietro Badoglio and his minions to preside over a victory banquet. It is said that Badoglio was able to celebrate the conquest of Ethiopia with a fine dinner of champagne and overcooked spaghetti.

Although the Italians succeeded in stopping the rioting and instilling some basic form of law and order, it must not be forgotten that they were also looters themselves. During the course of their occupation, the Italians procured much in the way of choice pieces of Ethiopian art and monuments. Anything that reflected the tradition of Ethiopia's long history and imperial legacy was up for grabs, especially since the Italians sought to replace Ethiopia's legacy with their own.

The residents who hailed from foreign countries were likely the most reassured by the Italian presence. This was not due to any great love of the Italians but more out of a basic instinct for survival. Just prior to the Italian occupation, non-Ethiopians were the most likely to be targeted in discriminatory reprisals by an angry and frustrated Ethiopian populace.

British journalist George Steer, who was on the ground at the time, experienced this sudden onslaught of xenophobic, anti-European hatred firsthand when a group of infuriated Ethiopians tried to seize him and his party during those frightful early days in May. This grim incident occurred on May 2nd in the ensuing power vacuum between the exit of the Ethiopian ruler and the advent of Italian occupation.

Steer described the following, "The streets were filled with smoke, the flames were running from shop to shop, cars which had crashed or been abandoned at the roadside were burning, hot black refuse in our way could be seen through the level glare of the descending sun and the harsh irritating breath of the furnace which started tears from our eyes. A few Ethiopians, in bands, hacked at the side of [our] lorry. In the waste setting of broken and flaming Addis Ababa with the telephone wires in tangled black nets dangling across the roadway, to the tune of shattered glass under our lorry wheels, their faces and the horrible lie of the straddled corpses looked too unbearably horrible."

Steer then went on to describe the effect of the strong-willed monarch's sudden exit, depicting him as a figure who seemed to control all of Ethiopia in the palm of his hand and how his exit ushered in absolute chaos. As Steer recalled, "Order here had been a flimsy thing, sustained by the superb will of a single individual. Its destruction, in a welter of fire, dirt, explosions, was suddenly visible in every sordid detail."

George Steer was an amazing journalist who captured incredible details of some of the most intense war zones around the world. As an interesting aside, it is ironic to note Steer's death. He survived the aforementioned chaos that had erupted in Addis Ababa, as well as several other hotspots of violence around the globe, only to perish in Burma on December 25th, 1944, not from an act of violence but in a car accident as he rushed off to a Christmas party.

As a result of the chaotic situation in the Ethiopian capital, the Italians were able to present themselves as protectors and peacemakers, even though they were the ones who had instigated all of these problems in the first place. Mussolini seemed to invoke this façade of the Italians as peacemakers when he gave his triumphant address to the Italian people on May 5th.

He stood on a balcony overlooking the Palazzo Venezia, declaring to an ecstatic crowd the virtues of Italian dominion over Ethiopia. He declared, "During the thirty centuries of our history, Italy has known many solemn and memorable moments—this is unquestionably one of the most solemn, the most memorable. People of Italy, people of the world—peace has been restored." He, of course, left out the inconvenient fact that Ethiopia was relatively peaceful before Italy decided to invade. But now that Mussolini had stirred up chaos, he was willing to take credit for bringing some sense of stability to the region.

Perception is everything, and initially, the Italians were quite good at winning over public opinion. It was really only after the start of World War Two, when Benito Mussolini became fully entrenched as Hitler's wartime ally, that the world mobilized against the Italian fascists. Prior to this, the pressure of German and Japanese threats was enough to stay their hand when it came to Italy's ambitions in East Africa.

However, after Britain and France were forced to declare war on Germany in 1939, all bets were off. The fact that Britain and France were locked in battle with Mussolini's buddy Hitler only served to encourage a stronger stand against Italy. It was after this point that Mussolini no longer had a free hand in Ethiopia.

Nevertheless, between 1936 and 1939, Mussolini seemed to have achieved a clear victory and a political coup. A few days after the triumphant entry of the Italians in Addis Ababa, the king of Italy, Victor Emmanuel III, was declared the new emperor of Ethiopia. King Victor Emmanuel III was a complicated figure; at times, he was in solidarity with and at other times at odds with his militant prime minister, Benito Mussolini.

In the telling of the story of wartime Italy, the role of the Italian king is often overlooked or overshadowed by the bombastic Benito, but it is important to highlight his role. Unlike Germany, which had only one sovereign leader in charge, Adolf Hitler, Italy was more complicated. Yes, Mussolini had a tight grip on power for some time, but his rule was not absolute.

When it was obvious that Italy's cause was lost, King Victor Emmanuel would ultimately have Mussolini sacked from his post as prime minister and arrested (before he was rescued in a daring German raid). In this regard, Italy's situation during World War Two was more similar to Japan than it was to Germany. Japan also had a sovereign monarch, Emperor Hirohito, who largely stayed in the shadows while his fascist prime minister, Hideki Tojo, oversaw the war on his behalf.

Similarly, Mussolini's power was never absolute, and all it took was a decisive downturn in Italian public opinion to end his career. But the triumph of 1936 and Prime Minister Mussolini's forced removal from office in 1943 were two very different ends of his complicated political career.

At the outset of the Italian occupation, Mussolini was, at least for a time, brimming with confidence in his schemes. This was indicated shortly after the occupation of Addis Ababa. Mussolini stood before a cheering crowd in Rome and declared simply, in his bullish and belligerent manner, "Ethiopia is Italian."

In other words, the Italian dream of linking its colony of Eritrea to its colony in Italian Somaliland by seizing Ethiopia momentarily seemed to have been realized. The Italians called this conglomeration of Eritrea, Ethiopia, and Italian Somalia Italian East Africa. However, turning Ethiopia into an extension of Italy would not be as easy as Mussolini claimed.

In Mussolini's faraway perch in Rome, he could only dream about Italian East Africa. The Italian viceroy administrated affairs on the ground in Italian-occupied Ethiopia. The first viceroy was Italian General Pietro Badoglio. General Pietro Badoglio had greatly frustrated General Rodolfo Graziani, who had been delayed by the vicious fighting in the east, by beating him to the Ethiopian capital.

General Pietro Badoglio was an interesting character. Badoglio was born in 1871 and actually fought in the failed Italian campaign of 1896. He had seen Italy's defeat at the Battle of Adwa with his own eyes. Badoglio likely could still recall the names of comrades killed in the battle. For him, the seizure of Ethiopia was personal.

Well, at least personal enough for him to cash in. Badoglio left at the end of May, but not before pocketing what amounted to over a million dollars from the Bank of Ethiopia. It is said that upon his return to Italy, he used this money to purchase a fine estate. The house was huge, and he used much of it to house his war trophies, a miscellaneous mishmash of stolen Ethiopian artifacts. If all of this were not enough for Badoglio's ego, he was even granted an honorary degree from the University of Pavia.

The praise of Pietro Badoglio was so great that one of the leading lights of fascism of the time, Roberto Farinacci, was heard to quip that "the only honor not bestowed upon Badoglio was that of Cardinal." Yes, one can only imagine the utter shame of the Catholic Church if they had caved to popular pressure and made Pietro Badoglio one of the pope's cardinals!

At any rate, after the crooked Badoglio's departure, the reins of power were handed over to Graziani. The official reason for Badoglio's return to Italy was allegedly a chronic heart condition that had become worse, but Graziani did not believe it and joked that Badoglio was simply seeking his "triumphs and honors" in Rome. Such a claim had truth in it; as mentioned, Badoglio was heaped with high praise and given many honorary titles upon his return.

In many ways, Badoglio was the favored son. He was able to indulge in the wartime glory of conquering Ethiopia, and after a very brief stay, he was able to return to Rome to claim his reward. Graziani was relegated to cleaning up the mess that Badoglio had left behind. Although Badoglio was at the head of the army that seized the Ethiopian capital, he did not stick around for the rebuilding and painstaking consolidation of these gains. This difficult task was left to Graziani.

As unpopular as the Italian occupation might have been, Graziani was a particularly unpopular administrator from the very beginning. Viceroy Rodolfo Graziani was a harsh taskmaster and sought to rule with an iron fist. His harshness would eventually come to haunt him on February 19th, 1937, when he was the target of an assassination attempt.

The incident occurred when Graziani was giving a rare public address to his Ethiopian subjects. The event, which was an alms-giving ceremony in which Italian administrators handed out money to waiting Ethiopians, was ostensibly supposed to create some sense of affinity among the new Ethiopian subjects. But despite the free cash that was distributed, Graziani did not present himself in the most endearing fashion.

The event was later recalled by an Ethiopian guard in the employ of the Italians, a certain Lieutenant Meleselin. He described the fenced-in platform from which Graziani spoke as thus, "Around the fence you could see those special guards fully armed with machine-guns, and looking as if they were hunting elephants." Within this cordoned-off ring of barbed wire and heavily armed troops, Graziani gave what amounted to a fascist stump speech in which he was seen ranting and raving with his arms in the air like some sort of mini-Mussolini.

The people in the crowd did not have a clue as to what he was saying, but the wild gestures were unnerving. As Meleselin recalled, "When we saw Graziani talking emotionally, throwing his arms in all directions, the veins visible on his neck, most of us stopped looking towards him and started to glance behind looking for an escape route."

As it turns out, the "escape route" that Meleselin sought would indeed be needed. In the immediate aftermath of the attack on Graziani's life, those guns would be mercilessly turned on the crowd of onlookers for apparently no other reason than the fact that they were there.

But we are getting ahead of ourselves. You must be wondering what exactly happened in the assassination attempt. Well, in the middle of this frenzied speech about the glories of Rome and fascism, someone in the crowd tossed a grenade onto the podium. Graziani was injured from the blast, but he would live, although this was not immediately clear at the time. Right after the blast, Graziani was knocked out and seen falling into a crumpled heap on the ground.

The Italian and the Ethiopian onlookers had two simultaneous reactions that would prove devastating. Upon seeing the stricken Graziani in the aftermath of the explosion, the crowd of Ethiopians, for the most part, became frozen to the spot, momentarily shocked into paralysis. The Italians behind the big guns had another reaction—they began opening fire.

Yes, they opened up those big guns Meleselin was so worried about and began to indiscriminately riddle the crowd with bullets. How terrible was this? The number of dead differ significantly, with the Ethiopians claiming thirty thousand died in the massacre, which lasted from February 19th to February 21st. The Italians saw upward to six thousand died. Regardless, the crowd had come out to be beneficiaries of the fascists' goodwill. Yet, after being given the alms from the Italians, they were filled with lead.

According to author Ian Campbell, who documented this event in his book, *The Addis Ababa Massacre*, of the few thousand Ethiopian citizens who were in attendance, it is believed that only a handful survived this ordeal. An eyewitness account from one of these few survivors, Temesgen Gebre, would later surface, shedding some light on just how awful this bloody spectacle was.

Gebre apparently survived because he was shielded by the dead corpses that fell on top of him. Another survivor was the aforementioned Lieutenant Meleselin, who would later describe his ordeal in rich detail. He talked about the moments immediately after the Italians opened fire, stating, "The dead fall upon the dead. Human blood streams like floodwater from the rain. The priests and the deacons fall to their death carrying the cross."

No one knew who had tossed the grenade, but all of the Ethiopians were considered suspects. As such, they were subject to a summary execution on the spot. Even Italian non-military personnel began seeking out Ethiopians to kill, picking up knives, shovels, clubs, trowels, or anything else on hand to finish off the Ethiopians.

These terrible acts were verified by an Ethiopian telegraph operator named Taddesse Zewelde, who bore witness to them. Zewelde would later recall the utter pandemonium, stating, "Those who were able to escape the courtyard were received by murderers holding shovels, axes, and hammers. They were beaten to death with such tools."

Another person who observed this mayhem, Kirubel Beshaw, similarly described the chaotic scene, saying, "A lot of people [who] were murdered after being repeatedly hit with big sticks, swivels, axes, hammers, stones or vehicle starting handles."

It is hard to imagine how the Italians could have suddenly turned on an entire people. In some ways, perhaps the first round of shooting, as bad as it was, was understandable. Considering that a bomb had just gone off, the notion that a few scared, panicky, trigger-happy troops might suddenly shoot into the crowd is in some ways predictable. While it can't be proven that the Italians planned to massacre the crowds of Ethiopians who had gathered that day, it seems they were fully prepared to unleash their weapons if and when they felt provoked. And they were ready to immediately leap upon any perceived provocation as a reason to do so. It is possible the Italians wished to commit war crimes regardless of what happened, but the bomb attempt gave them what they felt was adequate cover and reason to do so.

Yes, while we cannot know for sure, such things are not out of the realm of possibility. Then again, to say that what happened next was somehow part of a contingency plan of the Italian armed forces loses sight of the fact that the Italian soldiers were not the only ones to engage in conflict that day. Italian civilians also took part in the mob violence.

As the French envoy, Albert Bodard, who was there to witness this horrid episode of indiscriminate bloodshed, said, "Every Ethiopian was presumed guilty and had to be struck down." For those few who survived this melee, it really was a remarkable challenge just to stay alive. Many Ethiopians who survived were shipped off to prison camps, where the conditions were abysmal. Prisoners received the bare minimum of water and good and forced to toil on canals or plantations. Many died.

This synopsis of events after the attempt on Graziani's life was seconded by British diplomat William Bond, who similarly stated, "Wholesale executions followed at once in the grounds and adjoining field, and a large number of mere spectators, most of whom were entirely innocent, thus paid for their presence with their lives."

Another report on these war crimes from an Armenian resident of Addis Ababa, Edouard Garabedian, seems to demonstrate the seemingly spontaneous, organic nature of this outburst of violence. It is worth noting that Armenians, who are fellow Orthodox Christians, had a long relationship with Ethiopia. Almost since the capital city of Addis Ababa's inception, it has had an Armenian quarter. Garabedian was well acquainted with the city, and he knew the difference between an Italian soldier and an Italian civilian.

This was a point that Garabedian sought to drive home when he gave his account of the melee that ensued. Garabedian was shocked to see the same Italian civilians whom he had lived and worked with in the city delve into such demonic depravity. Garabedian would go on to state, "I saw them with my own eyes, beating every Ethiopian they met in the street with anything they could find. These Italians were civilians."

Even some Italian witnesses would later come forward and detail the bloodbath that took place. Among them was an Italian writer by the name of Ciro Poggiali. He was in a nearby hospital at the time due to a leg injury, but he heard the commotion that occurred. Although he had a bum leg, he forced himself to quickly head outdoors to see what was going on.

His eyes were immediately greeted by carnage and violence on a scale he had never imagined possible. He saw the fleeing Ethiopians being chased by mobs of infuriated Italians out for blood. As Ciro Poggiali described it, "All the [Italian] civilians in Addis Ababa had taken on the task of revenge, forming squads with lightning speed, in the most authentic squadristi manner." The term *squadristi* was used by the fascists quite a bit and referenced aggressive hit squads that were assembled to dish out the fascist brand of justice.

Interestingly, the words of an Italian writer, Ciro Poggiali, give us the most likely explanation of what had happened. Poggiali's account points to a terrible event that was not specifically planned for, yet it was something the Italian soldiers and Italian civilians had already been preconditioned to accept.

In his account, Poggiali reminds us of the mentality that the Italians had in occupied Ethiopia. Under the fascist regime, Italians in Ethiopia were routinely brainwashed by propaganda of how they needed to immediately form "revenge squads" to carry out swift vengeance (or, as Poggiali put it, "with lightning speed) on the Ethiopian populace should any Ethiopian stand in their way during a crisis situation.

The general approach of the Italian occupation, especially under the dreaded General Rodolfo Graziani, was to punish the Ethiopians as a whole, even if just one of them had transgressed. It seemed that once the Italian civilians were alerted to the failed attack, they took it upon themselves to carry out wholesale vengeance in the name of Italian fascism.

As a testament to just how committed the Italians were to this wretched cause, one Ethiopian man who survived this travesty, Mekonnin Denneqe, was actually working for the Italians as an interpreter when he came under direct threat. When push came to shove, Denneqe quickly realized that his distinction of being on the Italians' payroll no longer applied. Despite his previous loyal service, the vengeful *squadristi* was now at his heels, and his number one task was no longer translating for the Italians but running for his life.

He managed to reach the higher ground of the courtyard of St. Mark's Church, where he scaled a fence and was effectively able to hide out until the situation cooled down. But it would take a considerably long cooling-off period to chill the boiling blood of the wrathful Italians, especially those of the *squadristi*.

# Chapter 6 - Graziani Gets His Revenge

*"An enemy forgiven is more dangerous than a thousand foes."*

*-Rodolfo Graziani*

General Rodolfo Graziani was not killed in the blast that occurred in the spring of 1937. He was hurt, but he suffered no lethal wounds from which he could not heal. As he coalesced in his sickbed recovering, he began to formulate his plans for revenge. Graziani's subordinates were eagerly awaiting orders for more reprisals. They did not have to wait long.

While Graziani lay in a hospital bed recuperating, he issued orders for the fascist group the "Black Shirts" to be set loose upon the Ethiopian population of Addis Ababa. And in a series of indiscriminate reprisals, homes were razed, people were killed, and some were tortured. It is interesting to note that when Rodolfo Graziani was prosecuted after the war, he steadfastly denied being behind these orders.

During Rodolfo Graziani's trial in 1948, he argued that since he was laid up in the hospital at the time, there was no way he could have been behind the mayhem. His argument seemed plausible enough. He had just sustained injuries from a grenade and had been temporarily rendered unconscious.

It is certainly easy to argue that he was not capable of issuing commands in such an incapacitated state. But much of his claims of ignorance were proven false when documents with his own signature began to surface, specifically authorizing acts of punitive retribution shortly after the assassination attempt on his life.

Even more damning was the fact that Rodolfo Graziani issued an official proclamation to all of Italian-occupied Ethiopia in the immediate aftermath of the assassination. The proclamation detailed the assassination attempt and Graziani's orders for reprisal.

Rodolfo Graziani declared the following:

"On February 19th, while I was distributing alms to the poor, and contributing to the churches of Addis Ababa to celebrate the birth of His Highness the Prince of Naples, grandson of our great and powerful King and Emperor, Vittorio Emanuele II, a few rascals purchased with foreign gold made an attempt to kill me and the other great officials of the government. God, however, was willing to keep my life and the lives of the others who were with me, and [we] escaped with light wounds. Now justice is taking its course without interruption and decisions are being executed without mercy."

Even though Graziani omits the gory details, he openly admits that his orders were "executed without mercy." He also throws in some falsehoods, such as alleging the assassins were "purchased with foreign gold." In reality, they were disgruntled Eritreans on the Italian payroll!

Rodolfo Graziani also did not miss a chance to perpetuate the farce that the king of Italy was the rightful emperor of Ethiopia. It might have sounded good to him on paper, but no one really believed this to be the case. King Victor Emmanuel (Vittorio Emanuele) had enough problems at home and likely could have cared less about faraway Ethiopia at the time.

If he did, he would have probably been quite shocked to find that his newly acquired empire was literally going up in flames. Some of the worst atrocities committed during this period involved the systematic spraying of villages with gasoline and then setting them ablaze. This was all courtesy of the flamethrower-wielding fascist fanatics, the Black Shirts.

Historian and author Ian Campbell, who documented much of these atrocities in his book *The Addis Ababa Massacre*, described the Black Shirts as being largely made up of the lower ranks of Italian society. These were men who were typically looked down upon by the traditional elite in Italy. A good portion of them may have been ex-convicts who had been recently released from Italian prisons. Just prior to the war, a general amnesty had been issued for certain prisoners who pledged to join the fight.

The idea that there was a strong undercurrent of criminality among the Black Shirts is hard to argue with when looking at their actions. They commonly engaged in ruthless murder, the destruction of property, and theft, just to name a few.

It seems that many of the Black Shirts were former crooks back home in Italy, and as such, they were always on the lookout for something valuable to pocket. The wealthier Ethiopians, in particular, were targeted. Their lives might have been spared, and their home might not have been burned to ash, but more than likely, these thugs walked away with as much loot as they could if they happened upon their property.

According to Ian Campbell, upon reaching Ethiopia, many of these dregs of Italian society were exhilarated to find that not only did Italy's class distinction not apply to them in Italian-occupied Ethiopia but also that they were suddenly considered to be something special and set apart. As long as they showed their loyalty to the fascist cause (especially through acts of violence), they were considered valuable members of the fascist order.

Campbell contends these men were seduced by the cult of fascism. Seeking to enhance their status in the eyes of fascist leaders like Rodolfo Graziani, the Black Shirts eagerly tried to gain an advantage over each other. They wanted to prove themselves as being wholly committed to fascism by being as ruthless as possible.

This toxic environment fostered these flamethrower-wielding madmen, who torched homes with absolutely no concern whatsoever, even if the inhabitants were inside their homes at the time. The fascists coldly referred to these crimes as merely "cleaning up sections of the city." Cleaning it up by burning it down? Was Rodolfo Graziani like a modern-day Nero, fiddling while Ethiopia burned?

The sections that were burned were primarily outlying thatch cottages that had been erected on the outskirts of Addis Ababa. Roman Emperor Nero supposedly burned down sections of Rome so that he could rebuild them to his liking. Is this what General Rodolfo Graziani was doing? Along with wholesale reprisal, was he also burning down outlying sections of the city so that he could rebuild them?

Lending credence to this idea was the fact that Graziani and his goons took special care not to damage the sections of the city that they liked. The well-to-do neighborhood of Siddist Kilo, which had some of the nicest houses in the city, was left largely intact. This was not out of any sympathy for the residents but apparently because the Italians wanted to spare the more affluent dwellings. The cottages of the poor sections of town were deemed as eyesores and expendable.

Whatever the case may be, despite any attempt at the minimization of their atrocities, there is no way to hide the egregious abuse that occurred under the direct orders of the Italian viceroy. As Ethiopian scholar Bahru Zewde put it, "With official backing, the black shirts, the political zealots of the Fascist order, went berserk in the city, chopping off heads, burning down houses with their inhabitants, dissembling pregnant women and committing all manner of atrocities."

Somewhere in the midst of all of these terrible war crimes, the Italian authorities managed to capture the two men who were responsible for the attempt on Rodolfo Graziani's life. The assassination attempt had been made by two young men, Abraha Deboch and Moges Asgedom. Interestingly, these two were recent transplants to Ethiopia, having come from Eritrea.

The fact that these men hailed from the Italian colony of Eritrea rather than being from Ethiopia was extremely disconcerting to Italian officials. These men were basically viewed as being akin to spies since they were well acquainted with Italian bureaucracy. However, as it would be discovered, they were recruited by the local Ethiopian resistance to carry out an assassination against the viceroy.

Most concerning to the Italians was the fact that Abraha had even served as an employee at Graziani's own office. He had basically worked as an intelligence operative, collecting data on dissident Ethiopians. Yet, he had somehow been convinced to switch sides and strike at Rodolfo Graziani himself. One can only imagine the panic in the Italian ranks, as they began to see potential enemies and saboteurs everywhere they looked, both on the inside and outside.

Even after the two men were captured, the Italians sought to punish a whole community for what had happened. This punitive act would devolve into a terrible massacre and would stand out as one of the worst moments of the Italian occupation. According to Ethiopian scholar and historian Bahru Zewde, the attempt on Rodolfo Graziani's life and the aftermath of reprisals is quite significant.

Zewde asserts that the series of events that occurred in the spring of 1937 mark a solid demarcation between what he terms to have been the "first phase" of largely conventional warfare against the Italians and the "second phase" of underground, all-out guerilla warfare. To be sure, there was some mixture of both throughout the conflict, as official army regiments in remote regions suffered random ambushes from guerillas from time to time.

But after Graziani's attempted assassination, the whole situation changed. Rodolfo Graziani made it clear that he would no longer consider any Ethiopian freedom fighter as anything other than a criminal of the highest order who deserved the death penalty. In his mind, the Ethiopians were not fighting for their freedom, and anyone who dared defy Italian rule was an insurrectionist worthy of death.

The Ethiopian civilization was thousands of years old, but Rodolfo Graziani was expecting everyone to just give up and accept Italian rule without question. And despite knowing about the Geneva Convention doctrine on the treatment of prisoners of war, Graziani said that if any remaining Ethiopian fighters were captured in the field, they would not be spared but would face immediate execution. Most shocking of all, this happened even when they surrendered. Ethiopian regional warlords and siblings Abarra Kasa and Asfawasan Kasa were convinced to surrender to Italian forces, only to be shot on the spot as soon as they handed over their arms.

The game had clearly changed, and the Ethiopian resistance was forced to go further underground. As the war entered its second stage, guerilla warfare and the grim prospect that surrender would mean only death became the reality.

As one might imagine, the notion that giving up would only mean your death encouraged guerrilla fighters to fight even harder. They fought as if their very life depended on it—because it did. During the second phase of the resistance to Italian occupation, there would be no turning back, and there would be no surrender. The Italians would later realize the mistake they had made by further emboldening the resistance movement, but by then, it would be too late.

Rodolfo Graziani was hard to deal with before the attempt on his life, but he was most certainly even harder to deal with after it. And he was not only heavy-handed when it came to suspected saboteurs. His own subordinates often suffered the brunt of what has been termed his "neurotic" style of leadership. Others had a problem with Graziani's administration because he tended to give accurate reports as to the actual conditions on the ground.

And things were not going well in Ethiopia. An Ethiopian resistance movement referred to as the "Patriots" (known in the Ethiopian language as Arbegnoch) was established. The group was founded by a young Ethiopian nationalist named Abebe Aregai. Aregai was an interesting figure. He proved to be an excellent strategist and was able to lead successful ambushes against the Italians, even when his fighters lacked basic ammunition.

Under Aregai, a lack of supplies was not an excuse; it was a lack of imagination that he fumed against. No matter what the circumstances might have been, he found ways to repeatedly catch the Italians off-guard and beat them at their own game. Abebe Aregai was actually captured several times, but like some sort of magician, he was always able to escape.

Aregai would live to see Ethiopia's liberation and would play a role in the fighting that ushered in Haile Selassie's return. He would be greatly rewarded for his services. After the war, he was named the governor of Addis Ababa. After Aregai's tenure as governor came to a close, he would then be tapped as Ethiopia's minister of defense—a role that he knew more than a little something about.

It is with some strange irony to note that although Aregai had survived the long struggle against the Italians, he would be killed by one of his own countrymen when an attempted coup broke out in Addis Ababa in 1960. The coup was put down, but Aregai, the emperor's brave soldier who had long served with distinction, died from one of the rebel's bullets.

Along with organized armed resistance during the Second Italo-Ethiopian War, there was also intellectual resistance. Arbegnoch established the mouthpiece of the resistance, a newspaper called *Pillar of Light of Ethiopia*.

However, it would be inaccurate to say that all Ethiopians were suffering under the yoke of Italian rule. Some actually embraced it. And those who stood to benefit most were the average workers in the cities.

As soon as Italian industry roared to life, Ethiopians benefited by being hired on for well-paying jobs in the mad rush to build roads and other forms of infrastructure. They were paid more by the Italians than they ever were by Ethiopian Emperor Haile Selassie's regime. But even though the money was good, they would not be so easily bought off.

No matter what "improvements" the Italians promised, the Ethiopians were never going to rest until the Italian occupation was dislodged. And almost as soon as the Italian occupation began, the Italians were being harried by those hellbent on getting rid of them.

In the meantime, Italian troops were spread increasingly thin, placed in various *Bande* around Ethiopia. *Banda* (singular of *Bande*) is an Italian word that is actually slang for "gang," but in this instance, it was used to refer to a group of soldiers.

Interestingly, long after the Italians left Ethiopia, the *Bande* would be remembered. The word is one of the many loan words that have found its way into the Ethiopian language of Amharic. Just like Ethiopians use the Italian word *machina* for car, whenever they describe a gang of troublemakers, they refer to them as nothing but a bunch of *Bande*. This use of terminology was seen in the recent Ethiopian conflict in the northern province of Tigray, which erupted in 2021, in which Tigray rebels were often derisively referred to as *Bande*.

At any rate, life was certainly not easy for these Italian *Bande*. If they were to so much as step outside of the controlled zones of Italian occupation and into the outskirts of the cities, they would be open to ambush. One must remember that the Italian occupation of Ethiopia was an occupation of cities. The vast countryside would remain largely out of reach and be extremely dangerous for any Italian who happened to wander there.

This was demonstrated shortly after the Italian occupation of Ethiopia began when a distinguished general of Italy's air force, Vincenzo Magliocco, had to make an emergency landing in the countryside southwest of Addis Ababa. Resistance fighters on the ground were apparently watching the plane as it went down, and no sooner than it had come to an abrupt stop during its crash landing, hordes of warriors were on top of the craft, pulling out the survivors. They were not being pulled to safety, mind you, but to be brutally massacred. And this was the end of General Vincenzo Magliocco.

Such an event might seem like a fortuitous bit of luck on the part of the Ethiopian resistance since they just happened to be in the right place at the right time to devastate an Italian fighter plane and take out a high-ranking Italian official. But this might not have been a coincidence. The Ethiopian underground resistance movement developed its own sophisticated intelligence network, which was able to tip off resistance leaders to all kinds of events.

The resistance movement had its own agents who could pass between Italian-occupied territory and the wilderness that was swarmed with Patriots to divulge all manner of information. According to Bahru Zewde, this was largely the reason why the Italian air force was never able to achieve total dominance in the skies over Ethiopia since sharp-eyed intelligence operatives were closely monitoring all movements of Italian troops, both on the ground and in the air.

Of course, this was precisely what General Rodolfo Graziani had feared, and it was something he was trying to root out with his bloody reprisals. The Ethiopian Patriots had to be on their guard lest the Italians somehow infiltrate their network. They created their own form of security through a pass system. Their agents had to present special passes and identity papers confirming their status within the group to gain access. This underground intelligence network worked incredibly well, and no matter how hard the Italians tried, they could not infiltrate it.

Often enough, it was the very ineptness of Italian colonial rule that worked against them. It is said that the Ethiopian resistance was greatly encouraged by the lack of coordination within the Italian administration. For example, Italian Foreign Minister Alessandro Lessona was charged with assessing the state of affairs in Italian East Africa. He is said to have criticized Italian rule as often vacillating from being weak and ineffectual to being too strong and heavy-handed. In order to rule with at least some measure of respect from those you rule over, you have to have a steady hand.

Displays of weakness and overreach would not do the Italians any good. It is largely for this reason that the *Bande* became associated with being clownish bullies.

Besides the fact that militants were routinely attacking Italian troop positions, another serious problem was that there was a shortage of grain. Ironically enough, Ethiopia had been touted as being a future breadbasket for Italy. However, Italy bled the country dry of grain to feed the 500,000 some Italians who had relocated to Ethiopia! In 1936 alone, around seventy-five thousand tons of grain were delivered to Ethiopia from Italy. This transaction was carried out to the tune of some forty-three million Italian lire. In short, the promised boon of Ethiopia was rapidly turning into a financial disaster for Italy.

In many ways, everything about the Italian occupation of Ethiopia was a rushed, haphazard affair. The Italians had conquered a country with very little in the way of planning for what to do next. Sure, they established military garrisons in the major cities and instituted a military governor, but the civil structure of the occupation was always very weak.

Part of this could simply be due to the inability of Italian Prime Minister Benito Mussolini to make up his mind. It seems that Mussolini was never quite sure if he wanted to conquer all of Ethiopia or not. Even after the war had begun, there was still talk of just seizing a chunk of Ethiopia, perhaps just the northern provinces, and then coming to terms with an Ethiopian rump state led by the defeated Haile Selassie.

It is said that when Selassie was on his heels, ready to flee the country, Mussolini decided to conquer the country as a whole. If so, this mindset explains much when it comes to the lack of proper planning for Ethiopia's administration. Historian and scholar Alberto Sbacchi touched upon all of this in his book *Ethiopia under Mussolini: Fascism and the Colonial Experience.*

Here, Sbacchi drives home the point that Italian planners had not anticipated a direct Italian rule of Ethiopia but rather a rule through an Ethiopian puppet ruler, whether that puppet be Selassie or a suitable subordinate. This would have left the existing Ethiopian civil structure intact, saving the Italians the trouble of rebuilding a civil government from scratch. However, with the departure of Haile Selassie and his court, such plans were no longer feasible.

Even the occasional dialogue with remaining members of the aristocracy would not yield any beneficial fruit for the Italians in the vast power vacuum they had stepped into. It was not until 1940, when World War Two was already underway, that serious effort went into creating an effective colonial administration of the country.

At any rate, Rodolfo Graziani was not trying to hide any of these inconvenient facts from Benito Mussolini, which was quite different from other fascist flunkies who always pumped Mussolini up with false reports that everything was just fine. This is the fatal flaw of totalitarian fascist regimes in the first place.

Adolf Hitler's Germany would have very much the same problem in Europe, as subordinates did not wish to distress the Führer with bad news, sugarcoating every report to make things seem better than they were. This happened even when the Russians were breaking through German lines and threatening to head west toward Germany itself.

However, Rodolfo Graziani was not one to mince words, and he was sure to tell Mussolini what was really happening. Benito Mussolini seemed to prefer to see things through rose-tinted glasses, though, and he did not like all the negative reports he was receiving. At one point, he even complained that Graziani was writing him "too many letters."

Adding to Benito Mussolini's ire was the fact that Rodolfo Graziani threw protocol out the window when making his entreaties. Instead of lodging official complaints with the Department of the Ministry of Africa, he penned letters and sent various other documents directly to Mussolini himself.

With a little imaginative license, we can now imagine a very disgruntled Mussolini up early in the morning, a newspaper under his arm, checking his mailbox, only to be disgusted by the deluge of discouraging mail from Rodolfo Graziani. Perhaps Mussolini muttered under his breath, "What miseria! It's Graziani again!"

Shortly after these last attempts to enlighten Mussolini, Graziani packed up his bags and left Ethiopia altogether.

# Chapter 7 - Graziani's Exit— Fascism Gets a Facelift

*"Fascism, the more it considers and observes the future and the development of humanity, quite apart from political considerations of the moment, believes neither in the possibility nor the utility of perpetual peace."*

*-Benito Mussolini*

As much as Benito Mussolini complained about Graziani, he was typically a very duplicitous character in his political dealings. Italian diplomat and Mussolini's son-in-law Galeazzo Ciano documented as much when he made an entry in his diary for February 26th, 1938, which recalls Mussolini greeting the former viceroy and even giving him a hug even though Mussolini was all too quick to speak ill of Graziani behind his back Mussolini insisted that although he Graziani a good general, he was a terrible administrator.

After Graziani's exit from Ethiopia, he was ultimately succeeded by a much less brutal but still fascist viceroy named Amedeo Umberto, Duke of Aosta. At the time, Prime Minister Mussolini was concerned Italians were being portrayed too negatively in their occupation and expressed regret over Italians who had "acted badly." Therefore, he encouraged Amadeo Umberto's softer approach and even recommended that some of those Italians who "acted badly" be executed to demonstrate to the world that Italians still had a sense of honor.

Although the international community was slow to act, Mussolini's sudden concern is a clear indication that the world was taking notice of what Italy was doing in Ethiopia. One of the best advocates for shining a light on these atrocities was a member of Selassie's government-in-exile, Dr. Workneh Eshete.

Eshete was Ethiopia's foreign minister to London, and like Selassie, he had watched the developments in Ethiopia with horror from his diplomatic outpost in England. Eshete drew attention to the fact that the fascists had deemed anyone believed to be contrary to their rule as a dangerous subversive who could be executed for rebelling.

Eshete rightfully pointed out that although the Italians occupied a handful of cities, the war was not even over yet. There were still Ethiopian commanders in the field with intact armies fighting in the countryside. The notion that any soldier taken prisoner in the war could be summarily executed as a "subversive" merely for carrying on the fight against an invading country was a war crime.

Eshete then went on to point out that these measures would not only be applied to soldiers but also to civilians and basically anyone who just so happened to rub the Italian occupiers the wrong way. And if recent reports of what was happening in Ethiopia were not enough to make his case, Eshete pointed to what the Italians had already done to Libya.

In 1911, the Italians launched an unprovoked assault on Libya, which at that time was still part of the Ottoman Empire. Italy receives the credit of being the first nation to use aerial bombardment and to indiscriminately bomb soldiers and civilians from the air. This kind of mayhem was repeated in Ethiopia.

But the point that Eshete really wanted to drive home was the brutality of the subsequent Italian occupation of Libya. In his formal written protest, Eshete stated that during the course of the occupation, the Italians "disgraced and degraded themselves by committing shameful atrocities on their defeated opponents." He then went on to list the egregious abuses of both Libyan soldiers and civilians, which had strong parallels with what the Italians were doing in Ethiopia.

Mussolini was still trying not to get on France's and Britain's bad side, so he was concerned about how the Italian occupation was perceived. He had not yet forged his infamous axis with Germany and Japan. So, and this stage of the game, he was still attempting to obscure Italian atrocities.

Along with seeking cover for the heavy-handed administration of Ethiopia, Mussolini was also keen to stress the need for Ethiopia to be placed on sound economic footing. So far, by this point, Ethiopia had been more of a drain on the Italian economy than anything else. An unspoken part of this problem was the endemic corruption of Italian colonial officials, who pocketed more than their fair share of proceeds for themselves. Duke Amadeo Umberto would later complain that his subordinates in Italian East Africa were irredeemably inept and corrupt.

Interestingly, just prior to the attempt on Graziani's life, some efforts to work with the Ethiopian nobility had been made, even though it was highly debatable what benefit such things had for the Ethiopian elite. Their titles were meaningless, and by submitting to the Italians, they had lost much of the people's respect. However, even the meager connection between the Italian occupiers and the Ethiopian nobles was temporarily suspended in the immediate aftermath of the assassination attempt on Graziani.

Even though they likely had nothing at all to do with the incident, in Graziani's push for reprisal, many of the elite were actually deported to Italy as punishment. Their exile was a brief one. When Graziani's successor, Amadeo Umberto, came to realize that ruling Ethiopia was much easier by working through the Ethiopian nobility than through his own corrupt and inept cronies, they were restored.

It was hoped that Amadeo's approach would provide a reset between Italian Ethiopian relations, and for the most part, it did. He was seen as a much more clever and able administrator, and his willingness to work with local Ethiopian leaders was appreciated. Even Emperor Haile Selassie, who watched these developments from exile, had to admit that Amadeo was a good administrator. At one point, he stated that Ethiopia should be "grateful" for his kindness.

However, even though there were some leaders of the nobility who were willing partners of the Italians, there were also those who actively continued to carry out the resistance. Ras Imru held out until late 1936, when his shattered forces were cornered. Imru was the highest-ranking Ethiopian authority in the land after Selassie's departure. In fact, Imru had essentially been made Selassie's viceroy in his absence.

Considering the fact that so many others were killed upon their capture, it could very well be that the Italians recognized Imru's high rank and, therefore, purposefully kept him alive, perhaps thinking he might later serve as some sort of bargaining chip in the continuing conflict. Ras Imru was taken prisoner and was held as a prisoner of war for seven years on the Italian island of Ponza, which is somewhat ironic since that island was where Mussolini would be briefly imprisoned after he was first removed from office in 1943.

In the meantime, Ras Desta would continue struggling against the Italians until February 24th, 1937, when his army was similarly dismantled. Ras Desta was also captured. However, unlike Ras Imru, Desta would not be spared. He would be tried in a kangaroo court of Italians and then sentenced to death by firing squad. That year, 1937, would see massive uprisings and unrest in the far northern reaches of Ethiopia in parts of the country that the Italians had thought were secure.

Desta shortly before his execution.
https://commons.wikimedia.org/wiki/File:Ras_Desta_Damtew_as_prisoner_(1937).jpg

For instance, in Gondar around Lake Tana, Italian bases were stormed and captured (even if only temporarily), and the lives of Italian troops in the local garrisons were in significant jeopardy. Some of the outposts that were besieged were deemed to be so untenable that they were abandoned outright. This unrest would continue to spread sporadically in the Ethiopian Highlands.

One of the most notable rebel leaders in the final stages of the Italian occupation was Ras Abebe Aregai, who continued to fight the Italians on the periphery of their dominion. He used sound military tactics and political subterfuge to continue the struggle. This subterfuge was carried out by way of tacit talks of negotiations with the Italians. Ras Abebe famously used suggested peace talks as a means of an immediate ceasefire to build up his depleted forces.

He did this at the tail end of 1939 when he pretended to be willing to surrender. However, this was only a ruse to give him enough space to breathe new life into his nearly defeated force. And when he was ready to carry on the fight, he used the Italians' own brutal reprisals as an excuse to dismiss any notion of peace and reengage the Italians in the struggle to retake Ethiopia.

Although Ethiopia's true liberation would not come until 1941, when the British partnered with an Ethiopian force led by Haile Selassie, the relentless resistance put forth by rebel leaders like Ras Imru, Ras Desta, and the relentless Abebe Aregai kept the Italian rule weak and fractured, making Italy's ultimate defeat all the more imminent by the time of Haile Selassie's return.

# Chapter 8 – The Return of Haile Selassie

*"On this day which men on Earth and angels of Heaven could neither have foreseen nor known, I owe thanks unutterable by the mouth of man to the loving God who has enabled me to be present among you. Today is the beginning of a new era in the history of Ethiopia. Since this is so, do not reward evil for evil. Do not commit any act of cruelty like those which the enemy committed against us up to this present time. Do not allow the enemy any occasion to foul the good name of Ethiopia. We shall take his weapons and make him return by the way he came."*

*-Haile Selassie*

As much as an Italian victory seemed assured on the surface, thanks to the technological and numerical disparities between Italian and Ethiopian armed forces, Mussolini, despite all of his bombast and rhetoric, had moments where he doubted an easy victory. It is said that as late as February 1936, he was sending out feelers to Haile Selassie to see if a negotiated settlement could be reached.

The terms of these settlements could not have been anything that the Ethiopian monarch would have considered. The terms typically involved the Italians cutting off huge swathes of Ethiopian land in the north and east to create their desired land bridge, rendering Ethiopia a rump state of its former self. In exchange for this, Mussolini claimed he would recognize Ethiopian independence. But who could take the word of this Italian dictator?

To sweeten the deal, Mussolini threw in the port of Assab, a port that would give Selassie access to the Red Sea, something that the Ethiopian monarch had long sought. But, of course, this deal was no deal. Emperor Selassie would never agree to such a thing. Instead, he fought until the last minute and then was forced to flee his own country. He had to seek higher international ground to rally the world to Ethiopia's cause.

As we talked about above, Selassie spoke before the League of Nations, detailing Italian atrocities. He spoke of how the Italians used chemical weapons against Ethiopian troops in battle and how they had outfitted several planes with chemical sprayers so they could routinely fly over the Ethiopian countryside, spreading poisonous gas over "cattle, rivers, lakes, and pastures." The notion that the Italians were so desperate for a victory that they were willing to gas whole populations was and is chilling to contemplate.

But considering ruthless Italian General Rodolfo Graziani's own remarks before the war commenced, speaking of how he was going to deliver Ethiopia to Mussolini either "with or without the Ethiopians," one should not be too surprised. The Italians committed egregious war crimes not just against Ethiopian soldiers but also against the Ethiopian people as a whole.

The exiled emperor of Ethiopia stood before the League of Nations in Geneva, Switzerland, the august body that was put together to prevent such trespasses, and demanded action from the international community. Selassie reminded them, "It is the very existence of the League of Nations. It is the confidence that each state is to place in international treaties. In a word, it is international morality that is at stake. Have the signatures appended to a treaty value only in so far as the signatory powers have a personal, direct and immediate interest involved?"

He then concluded his remarks by warning those assembled that if they did not stop this spate of fascist aggression, they would be next. And when Hitler's tanks began rolling into Poland in 1939, many began to see the prophetic wisdom of Selassie's words. That very year, Ethiopia saw the first hints of outside intervention when Republican veterans of the Spanish Civil War, who had fought a losing battle against the forces of fascist Francisco Franco, decided to deploy to Ethiopia.

Ironically, Mussolini's very support of Franco nearly led to a conflict with Britain in 1938. It is without question that the British did not like

Italy meddling in Spain. But after a discussion with Prime Minister Neville Chamberlain, Mussolini found a way to appease the British prime minister by promising to pull his so-called Italian "volunteer troops" from Spain.

These volunteers hailed from the Black Shirts, the same group of fascists that had been terrorizing Ethiopia. Mussolini agreed to pull them out as long as the British did not place fortifications on the Mediterranean island of Cyprus and did not interfere with Italian aims in Ethiopia.

However, much of this pledge would be forgotten when the Italians aggressively invaded Albania in the spring of 1938. Even though the League of Nations seemed willing to wash its hands of Ethiopia, it could not ignore this. The League saw Spain and Albania fall to fascism like dominoes. And by the outbreak of World War Two, with Germany's invasion of Poland, the lines had been clearly drawn.

Although it's an often-forgotten chapter in Ethiopian history, Spanish freedom fighters, fresh from fighting fascist Black Shirts in Spain, briefly lent their support to the struggle against the Italians. And for what it was worth, a larger coalition of anti-fascist forces was slowly but surely taking shape.

In the meantime, Selassie set up shop in Bath, England. He used what remained of his resources to buy a nice, large house, which would form the seat of his government-in-exile. For the most part, Selassie was treated by the British as an exiled head of state. To Mussolini's chagrin, Selassie was even a guest of honor at the crowning of King George VI in 1937.

From his perch in Bath, Haile Selassie watched his own predictions regarding the consequences of the League of Nations' inaction come to pass. The League was slow to act. In fact, even the feeble sanctions they had imposed on Italy were removed just a few weeks after Selassie's impassioned address.

Even so, Ethiopia's struggle, which was once isolated and remote, would quickly become the struggle of the whole free world against the tyranny and oppression of fascism. In the late 1930s, the British, who were already on guard against German and Italian divisions encroaching upon British territory in Egypt, began to fear an Italian incursion in Sudan. The Italians had been preparing for such a contingency ever since declaring their solidarity with the Germans. Mussolini issued a secret order on March 31ˢᵗ, 1940, which made Sudan a prime target for Italian intervention.

The main concern for Italian troops on the ground was supplies. Their stocks had been used up in the war with Ethiopia, and the only way to actively replenish them was through delivery by plane or by crossing the Red Sea. And now that Britain was in the war against Italy, both of these routes were full of danger. As such, for the commanders on the ground, the most pragmatic strategy was for them to secure what limited resources they still had at their disposal and take a defensive position against any potential threats.

As the war heated up, it seemed as if a conflict between the Italians and the British in East Africa was all but inevitable. British controlled Kenya, which bordered Ethiopia to the south, and the British controlled Sudan, which bordered Ethiopia to the north.

Sudan shares a large northwestern border with Ethiopia. Ethiopian freedom fighters had long been crossing into Sudan for refuge. The British began to work with and train these Ethiopian fighters, creating the so-called "Gideon Force," which included Ethiopian, British, and local Sudanese fighters.

The British were preparing for what they now saw as an inevitable conflict with the Italians in East Africa. And on June 12ᵗʰ, 1940, they abruptly clued Haile Selassie in on their plans. After this impromptu debriefing, Selassie agreed to head to Khartoum, Sudan, to take part in the training of a revitalized liberation army.

It is worth noting that the opinion of British army officers both in regard to Selassie and the notion of a restored Ethiopia was sometimes skeptical. A certain Colonel H. C. Brocklehurst, who was under the command of British General Wavell, was often heard voicing his opinion that sections of Ethiopia should be partitioned and clumped together with other portions of already existing British colonies. Just like the Italians, these British officers were speaking of reducing Ethiopia to a rump state, relegated to just the central highlands around Addis Ababa while carving out a greater Kenya, larger Somalia, and grander Sudan.

Still, others were skeptical of the exiled Ethiopian emperor, Haile Selassie. Many could not wrap their minds around the notion that Haile Selassie had chosen to be absent from his own capital over the past few years and would be able to be successfully restored to the throne. They viewed him as nothing more than a "gimmick," as someone with no real importance to the actual war effort. Nevertheless, plans for the full liberation, plans that included Haile Selassie as an integral part, moved forward, regardless of these naysayers.

As Italians noted the troop buildup that was taking place with increasing alarm, they finally decided to roll the dice and launch a preemptive attack on British positions. On July 4th, 1940, Italian troops stormed into the Sudanese city of Kassala, just over the Ethiopian border. This was an important strategic position that the Italians wished to maintain in order to block access to their colony in Eritrea.

The attack was launched on July 4th at around three in the morning and consisted of three columns of Italian troops said to consist of some 6,500 soldiers. Kassala was very sparsely defended by just five hundred members of the British-assembled Sudan Defense Force (SDF). The SDF was fully aware of the methods of Italian bombardments, so the men ducked and covered during the initial onslaught of the attack, with Italian warplanes flying overhead.

The SDF then emerged and fought the Italians with fury, leading to the destruction of six tanks and many Italian casualties. However, by that afternoon, it was clear that the larger Italian force was going to win the day, and the SDF conducted a strategic retreat. It was a hard-won victory for the Italians, and they would soon come to regret it.

One must understand that the Italians at this time were hoping that the Germans would quickly knock the British out of the war, just as they had done to the French. The French had been defeated in May 1940, and the Germans had since begun bombarding Britain in an air war that would become known as the Battle of Britain, which would take place from July to October 1940. If Britain had been defeated by the Germans, the situation in Africa would have played out much differently. In such a scenario, one can imagine the defeated British having to come to humiliating terms just like the French. This would have allowed the Italians to prey upon British possessions in North Africa in a similar that the Japanese preyed upon French possessions in Southeast Asia.

But of course, the German armed forces, despite their best efforts, were not able to defeat Britain as Mussolini had hoped. The British survived the German bombardment, and a German plan for an amphibious invasion of Great Britain, which had been dubbed Operation Sea Lion, was scrapped. The British now had breathing room to recover and would soon be able to take out their wrath on the Italians.

In November 1940, British and Italian forces around Kassala once again collided. The Italians were initially successful in holding them back, with much of the credit once again going to their air power in the region. But the British resolve, which had been reluctant before, was growing stronger by the hour.

And not everyone among the Italians was blind to this fact. As early as December of that year, an Italian general by the name of Gustavo Pesenti began openly speaking about seeking an armistice with the British. He was fired for his defeatist attitude, but after the war, he began to be seen as a forward-thinking man, almost a veritable prophet, for the beginning of the end of Italy's occupation of East Africa was at hand.

In January 1941, the Gideon Force, consisting of newly trained and organized British and Ethiopian troops, drove forth from British holdings in Sudan and rolled right into the already war-weary Italians. The fact that the Italians had never completed their attempted subjugation of Ethiopia must be stressed. The Ethiopian resistance had continued in various forms, and the Italians were already worn down from this constant warfare, which took place on multiple fronts.

So, when this fresh group of freedom fighters arrived on the scene, the beleaguered legions of Italians were a much less formidable force than they would have been if the Ethiopians had stopped resisting. Because of the continued internal struggle against the Ethiopian resistance, the Italians were ultimately too tied down and distracted to put up a proper fight when they faced an invading army. As Ethiopian scholar and historian Bahru Zewde put it, "The resistance as a whole had a corrosive influence on Italian rule, both physically and psychologically."

Although Haile Selassie played an exceedingly weak hand, he had played it quite shrewdly. And now, Haile Selassie, like some avenging angel, had returned to the field of battle. Along with the leadership of Selassie, the Gideon Force was directed by British generals Daniel A. Sanford and Major Orde Charles Wingate.

Major Orde Charles Wingate was widely known as a brilliant strategist and a brilliant personality. Major Wingate was a very cultured and intelligent man, and he had a genuine passion for restoring the independence of Ethiopia and the millennia-old Ethiopian monarchy. Some thought Selassie was just a "gimmick," but Major Wingate was the first to correct them on how important Emperor Haile Selassie truly was.

In the midst of this onslaught of freedom fighters, the weak Italian foothold in Kassala fell on January 19th, 1941. Eager liberation army troops then poured into Eritrea, just as the Italians had feared, and began their long drive all the way to Addis Ababa. Before doing so, they made a brief pitstop. The group stopped just over the Ethiopian border, just in time for Haile Selassie to raise the Ethiopian flag.

Haile Selassie was now back on Ethiopian territory after years of exile, and he wanted to officially commemorate it. This celebration was not disturbed by the Italians. In fact, this piece of territory had already been secured by the Ethiopian resistance, and the Italians would not dare step near it. The group then moved in a large convoy some three hundred miles before stopping at what was termed an oasis known as the "Elephant's Water Hole."

Here, free of any Italian aggression, Emperor Haile Selassie found time for some fishing. It is said that he expertly netted several fish, which were then made into an enjoyable meal. After departing the Elephant's Water Hole, the journey became more dangerous, not necessarily because of the Italians. The forces faced rugged terrain as they advanced.

With no viable paths for mechanized transport, the group had to travel by horse and by foot to their next major destination, the city of Debra Marcos in the region of Gojjam. Haile Selassie entered this city on April 6th, 1941, after the Italian-backed administrator, Ras Hailu, gave up without a fight.

In the meantime, another British/Ethiopian contingent poured in from the south by way of British holdings in Kenya. In a wide flanking maneuver, the British under General Sir Alan Cunningham launched an assault on Italian Somaliland, seeking the same destabilizing maneuver that the ill-fated Ras Desta had tried yet failed to achieve back in 1935. Desta and his group were mercilessly blasted by Italian warplanes with no recourse to counter them. Fast forward to 1941. With the help of British arms and air support, the playing field had finally been leveled, and the Ethiopian and British soldiers were able to mow down the Italians like weeds.

Cunningham's contingent was then able to take the city of Mogadishu without much resistance as the Italians fled to the higher ground of the Ethiopian city of Harar. British and Ethiopian forces chased the Italians out of Harar, and they fled farther into the interior. As planned, the Italians were being herded into the center of the country, where they would be trapped with no hope of escape.

British and Ethiopian forces in both the north and the east were on the move, hurrying to Addis Ababa to liberate the embattled Ethiopian capital. Since the British had gained control of both Eritrea and Italian Somaliland, the Italian forces that had been chased into the interior were completely deprived of their supply lines. Realizing the situation was hopeless, Italian occupation forces fled Addis Ababa on April 6th (the very day that Selassie entered Debra Marcos) and literally headed for the hills.

Duke Amedeo, the able administrator whom Haile Selassie himself had once praised, was also chased out. Although the duke suffered from ill health, he proved that he was no coward. He had the opportunity to evacuate to safety beforehand but decided to stay with his subordinates. The beaten and battered Italian troops holed up in the mountains were now waiting for the end, whether that end came by way of an official end of the war or the end of their lives in a final stand-off against the British.

Ultimately, the duke would be captured at the Battle of Amba Alagi, which took place in May of 1941. Amba Alagi is one of the mountains that the Italians holed up in, and it was where Duke Amedeo made his last stand. He rallied what remained of his personal fighting force and prepared for a long stand-off.

As desperate as these efforts might seem, there was some strategic sense behind these actions. The mountain had many openings in which stockpiles of ammunition and other supplies could be stored. And once troops were in place around the natural fortifications of the mountain, it would be very difficult to dislodge them.

The first army of Ethiopian liberators to reach Amba Alagi was a battalion led by British General Mosley Mayne, who approached the mountain from the northern frontier on May 4th. General Mayne was joined by General Dan Pienaar's 1st South African Brigade, which arrived on May 12th. The reinforcements then kept on arriving until they managed to form a solid ring around the whole mountain by May 14th.

A massive assault was planned for the 15th, but these plans were rendered entirely unnecessary when a stray shot managed to blast into the Italians' fuel supplies, sending gasoline into the only source of drinking water the holed-up Italians had. With the scorching Ethiopian sun giving the parched and thirsty Italians no relief, they quickly realized they were absolutely doomed without a proper water supply. As such, they began entering into talks for surrender.

This surrender was made official, and as mentioned, Duke Amedeo Umberto was taken into custody. And he would live out his last couple of years of life as a prisoner of war. Despite his previous honor and distinction, this member of royalty would ultimately perish in a prisoner-of-war camp in British-controlled Nairobi, Kenya, in January 1943.

Although it might seem a bit suspicious that he perished in British custody like this, it seems that his demise was due to his previous health problems, which included bouts of malaria, dysentery, typhus, and even tuberculosis. All of these health issues were, no doubt, greatly exacerbated by the bleak conditions and limited resources of a prison camp.

At any rate, even with the main occupation forces destroyed, the last of the Italian holdouts would not be entirely defeated until November 27th, 1941, when Italian General Guglielmo Ciro Nasi surrendered the last Italian army group.

Haile Selassie had reached the capital on May 5th, 1941. However, his restoration to the Ethiopian throne was not immediate. It was likely a source of high anxiety for those eager to return the monarch to power, but the British dithered.

Citing security reasons, the British insisted that they run the show for a short period of time, leaving the country in a state of transitional martial law under British agency. As a result, there were those who feared that the Ethiopians had just traded an Italian occupation for a British one.

But the British insisted that these measures were temporary, and they ultimately kept their word. Even if they wanted to keep part of Ethiopia for themselves, after World War Two came to a close, such a proposition was no longer tenable. The battered and weary British, with their faltering war-shocked economy, could not hang onto the colonies they already had, let alone acquire a new one.

And as former British colonial territories, such as India, Pakistan, and Burma, were shaken loose from Britain's grip, the British quickly arranged Ethiopia's complete and utter restoration as well. Yes, despite all of the odds, at long last, Emperor Haile Selassie returned to the throne, and his empire was fully restored.

# Chapter 9 – Understanding the War and Its Repercussions

*"Throughout history, it has been the inaction of those who could have acted; the indifference of those who should have known better; the silence of the voice of justice when it mattered most; that has made it possible for evil to triumph."*

*-Haile Selassie*

Upon his return to Ethiopia, Haile Selassie surprised the world with his forgiving attitude toward the Italians who had ravaged his country. Upon his reinstatement, he famously gave a speech in which he urged his people to "not reward evil for evil" and not to "commit any act of cruelty like those which the [Italians] committed." These noble commands are right out of the Bible and perhaps would be a challenging thing to keep for many placed in such a difficult situation.

But nevertheless, in many ways, the Ethiopian people held up their part of the bargain. Reprisals against the Italians after the war were not common. Incredibly enough, many Italians chose to remain in Ethiopia rather than return to face the wrath of Mussolini after they were defeated in 1941. They apparently feared him more than they did the Ethiopian people.

If one were to travel to Ethiopia today, it would not take long to discover that a certain affinity for Italians exists there. Italian words and Italian food have become permanently intermixed with Ethiopian culture. It is not at all uncommon today to find a restaurant in Ethiopia serving injera (flatbread) with a hearty side of pasta. And no one thinks much of it. But the fondness for Italian fare is surprising considering all of the potential for animosity over past grievances.

Some are perplexed by how Ethiopians view Italy and Italians and have likened it to a kind of "love/hate" relationship. Despite the apparent differences between the Italian civilization and the Ethiopian civilization, they have pursued similar trajectories in their corresponding histories. Both are rooted in ancient civilizations that built massive empires long ago, and both saw their empires shrink and contract. The Roman Empire, of which Italy is an inheritor, once circled the entire Mediterranean, including large chunks of the Middle East and North Africa. The Ethiopian Empire was also once quite extensive, reaching all the way across the Red Sea and into Yemen. Both the Romans (or the Italians) and the Ethiopians were early adopters of Christianity. They both wholeheartedly embraced the religion in the 4th century, long before many other world powers even considered doing so. However, a big difference between the two is that the Roman Empire fell apart, yet the Ethiopian Empire was still going strong at the time of Mussolini's invasion.

The Italians were essentially seeking to destroy an already existing empire in their vain effort to revive the Roman Empire. The Italians and the Ethiopians both hailed from ancient and rich cultures, yet one was trying to forcibly overtake the other. But Selassie urged the Ethiopian people to embrace forgiveness and mercy rather than bitterness and animosity. And that was the path the majority of Ethiopians took.

There was not any grand Ethiopian movement to seek revenge against Italy. In many cases, the postwar attempts to right some of the wrongs that Italy inflicted on Ethiopia was a joint effort by both parties. One of the most recent was a joint effort by both Italian and Ethiopian activists to repatriate stolen artifacts that had been taken from Ethiopia during the war. The most famous of these was the Axum Obelisk (a 1,700-year-old artifact) that was returned to Ethiopia in 2005.

So, while there still is generally not much of an appetite for vengeance against Italy as a nation, there is a certain amount of wariness as it pertains to the continued legacy of Italian involvement with Ethiopia. And this wariness is most poignantly on display as it pertains to the children of Italian men and Ethiopian women. Ever since the days of the war, children from Italian and Ethiopian unions have faced a certain kind of stigma.

Even if a child of an Italian parent is born and raised in Ethiopia, they often find it very difficult to be fully accepted as *Ethiopians*. They could be Ethiopian in all the ways that matter, but if their first or last name is Italian, they are inevitably viewed as *ya-hulatt bandira leg*, or "children of two flags." Offensive terms are still used to describe someone of mixed heritage in Ethiopia today.

Some Italian-Ethiopians might take it all in stride, and others might take tremendous offense to it. And the context is likely very important if and when such terms are applied. If a friend comes up to an Italian-Ethiopian and uses the term, the two friends might laugh it all off, enjoying the absurdity of it all. But if such a word is hurled at someone in anger, the situation and the feelings that it would produce would be entirely different.

But at any rate, such things are a direct and lasting consequence of the Italian occupation. So, while Ethiopians generally do not wish for revenge against Italy or Italians, there is a kind of sarcastic remembrance in Ethiopian culture of Italy's role in the occupation of Ethiopia. And this sarcastic remembrance bubbles up to the surface from time to time in everyday life in the country.

But despite the potential for such lingering feelings of resentment, there has also been a lingering affinity for all things Italian. Italian clothes, culture, and food have long had a soft spot among Ethiopians. Ethiopians love Italian food; it is one of the most popular cuisines in the country. As mentioned, it is not at all uncommon to see Ethiopian restaurants serving up injera with heaping piles of pasta. Regardless of any past grievances, such fare is readily eaten without leaving a bad taste in anyone's mouth.

Yes, what the Italians did was wrong. They invaded a sovereign nation and committed war crimes against soldiers and civilians. There is no doubt about that. But even in the face of all of the evil they perpetrated, they did some good as well. They famously built miles and miles of roads and achieved great feats of architectural engineering during their brief occupation of the country. Some have indeed gone as far as to note that the Italians of this period seemed to be much better engineers than they ever were soldiers. The roads and infrastructure they built can still be seen today.

As noble as Haile Selassie's words were, there was a hint of pragmatism in them as well since the Italians who built all of these modern marvels that Emperor Selassie now had in his possession were the best equipped to service and maintain them. And Italian engineers would continue to work on Ethiopian infrastructure, not as invaders but as hired hands, over the next several decades.

It is also important to note how the Italians actually aided the Ethiopian economy (perhaps inadvertently) by nationalizing Ethiopian trade. Prior to the Italian occupation, certain groups within the country had a monopoly over trade. Much of it was carried on by foreign transplants. Bahru Zewde cites the most common traders in the Ethiopian market prior to the Italian invasion hailing from Yemen, not Ethiopia.

However, the Italians established the Mercato in the Ethiopian capital of Addis Ababa. The Mercato, which remains a famed tourist attraction to this day, is an open-air market in which Ethiopians can come and trade their goods without a middleman. Even though the Italians struggled to make a profit while they were in Ethiopia, almost immediately after their departure, the Ethiopians began to utilize the Mercato with great vigor. These developments led to the establishment of the Ethiopian National Corporation or ENC for short.

The ENC was able to nationalize the goods that flowed through the Ethiopian marketplace and arranged the selling of mass quantities of grain to the struggling countries of Europe both immediately before and immediately after the end of the Second World War. This distribution of grain was much appreciated in struggling Europe, and it was a great boon to Ethiopia as well. According to Zewde, the profits for 1944 alone were in the millions of dollars.

As money was being made from grain, a literal gold mine was found in the town of Adola in the Sidamo region, which is said to have brought in a fifth of the government's revenue that same year. In recognition of this feat, the town of Adola had its name changed to Kebra Mengest, which in Amharic means "glory of the government."

Yes, even though the Italians could not find a way to make money out of Ethiopia, as soon as they were kicked out, the Ethiopians most certainly did! Not bad at all for a country still struggling to reassemble itself after being occupied for five years by enemy forces. So, even though the Italians were to blame for Ethiopia's woes, there was still some benefit that could be derived from the occupation.

Nevertheless, the apparent leniency Emperor Haile Selassie had toward Ethiopia's former foes did not sit well with everyone. And the fact that the British, at least in the first few years of Selassie's return, kept the emperor on a tight leash also did not sit well with people. As previously mentioned, Emperor Selassie agreed to give the British nominal control while he crafted a new government, and many feared the British would simply pick up where the Italians had left off, becoming colonial overlords with Selassie as their puppet.

Selassie also had problems with some of his most powerful subordinates. There were regional rulers who had stuck out the fight with the Italians until the bitter end that were not so thrilled with Haile Selassie's sudden return. To them, he was a cowardly leader. They believe that Selassie did not deserve praise. Rather, they thought he should be scorned, and they refused to consider him their emperor.

Regional ruler Kidane Askale held animosity toward Haile Selassie because he blamed the emperor for the death of Menelik's heir, Lij Iyasu. In order to understand this situation, one needs a bit of a backstory. You see, the former Ethiopian monarch, Menelik II, had a grandson named Lij Iyasu, whom he had designated as his heir. Menelik passed away in 1913. Before Iyasu could secure his grip on power, much intrigue had erupted against him.

The biggest rumor that the Ethiopian nobles spread about Lij Iyasu was that he was secretly a Muslim. For Christian-dominated Ethiopia, this was a very big deal. In the modern day, where most of the world embraces religious freedom, we might not understand the importance of . such a thing, but in zealously Christian Ethiopia, any delineation from the traditional Christian faith would have been considered tantamount to treason.

Ethiopia had long been surrounded by Islamic neighbors in Somalia, Sudan, and Egypt. It had fought wars to maintain its long-standing Christian traditions, so a ruler accused of being a Muslim would have been viewed with deep suspicion. These suspicions were deepened when Iyasu selected a Syrian Muslim, Habib Ydlibi, to be his chief advisor.

But the real uproar occurred a short time later. After the outbreak of World War One in 1914, Iyasu seemed to suggest an interest in supporting the Ottoman Empire, which, along with Germany and Austria-Hungary, was part of the Central Powers. This alliance took on the British, French, Russians, and ultimately the Americans (known as the Allies collectively) in the war. Since the Ottoman Empire was an ancient Islamic state that had ruled much of the Middle East and North Africa for hundreds of years (the Ethiopians fought the Ottomans under Dawit II in the 1500s), Iyasu's opponents were horrified to see Iyasu once again courting the forces of Islam.

Even worse than the regional shock was the international blowback. When the Allied countries realized what Iyasu had in mind, they put an arms embargo on Ethiopia. They did not do this because they did not want the Ethiopians to support an Islamic polity such as the Ottomans but because they did not want Ethiopia to fall into the camp of the Central Powers.

It is important to take note of the embargo that Iyasu had inadvertently created during World War One. This trend of arms embargos, which lasted all the way up until the Italian invasion of 1935, would help to stunt Ethiopia's ability to wage war.

At any rate, all of this intrigue about Iyasu's allegiances, both personal and international, would ultimately do him in. In a virtually unprecedented move, the Ethiopian state and church acted in concert with each other to have Iyasu excommunicated, deposed, and placed into political exile. This is what led to Menelik's daughter Zewditu being given the crown and Ras Tafari (Haile Selassie) being made her regent before he took the throne and was crowned Emperor Haile Selassie in 1930.

Iyasu was placed under house arrest and had a heavy guard surveilling him. He remained under house arrest until he abruptly perished in November 1935. To this day, no one is quite sure what happened to him or how he died. But since his death occurred right at the outset of the Italian invasion, it has long been suspected that Haile Selassie ordered his execution.

If we make ourselves forget the cold-blooded nature of such a killing, pragmatically speaking, it would make sense. Just prior to Iyasu's demise, the Italians were plotting to somehow get Iyasu back on the throne as their puppet. They wanted to rule through him or, at the very least, use the notion of such a possibility as a means to stir up as much discord and dissent as possible.

On the eve of the war, the Italians, knowing full well the drama over Iyasu, dumped a bunch of propaganda tracts over Ethiopia. The tracts stated that Iyasu was the rightful emperor and that Ethiopians should rise up to overthrow Selassie and put Iyasu back on the throne. It was in the backdrop of all of this drama that Iyasu mysteriously perished. It could have been a coincidence, but many did not think it was.

One of those who had doubts was the aforementioned regional commander Kidane Askale. Practically as soon as Haile Selassie returned in 1941, Askale was saber-rattling against him. Haile Selassie had to lean on the support of the British to curtail this threat to his rule.

Selassie also had a problem with the so-called "Imru Party," which had rallied behind the exiled Ras Imru, arguably one of the most heroic and daring Ethiopian commanders in the war. This faction supported Imru and wished for him to become the next emperor of Ethiopia.

Even worse, there were also factions that were still supporting the remnants of the Italian occupation that had not yet been removed. These factions were certainly in the minority, but they were considerable enough to still present multiple thorns in Haile Selassie's side. And due to all of this pushback against Selassie, it very well could be argued that if it were not for the British backing him, Selassie might have found it next to impossible to return. But as all the necessary chips fell in place, one could consider that Haile Selassie was an ingenious strategist, extremely lucky, or that divine providence was at work because, despite all of the incredible odds against him, Emperor Haile Selassie was indeed restored to the throne.

There was still much that needed to be sorted out, including the fate of the former Italian colony of Eritrea. The region of Eritrea has a long and complicated history. Even the question of what is Eritrea is a loaded one that will bring forth multiple answers.

Eritrea was originally a part of Ethiopia, but it was carved off long ago by invading armies. The Ethiopians' old nemesis, the Ottoman Empire, controlled a large portion of it in the 16th century. The Italians came along in the 19th century and purloined their own piece of the colonial pie by seizing Eritrea for themselves.

They then infamously used their holdings in Eritrea as a gateway and a launching pad to make further inroads into Ethiopia proper. After the Italians' crushing defeat at the hands of Menelik II's forces at the Battle of Adwa, it would have made a whole lot of sense for the Italians to give Eritrea back to Ethiopia for all of the trouble they had caused. But the European powers were calling the shots and seemed to think that the

Italians had suffered enough. They refused to back such a concession.

However, the second time around, the terms that were imposed were much harsher than in the days of Menelik. The world was absolutely aghast at the fascist axis of Germany, Italy, and Japan and was not in the mood for any leniency. Italy would be stripped of all of its colonies, and Eritrea would come under British administration directly after the Italian defeat in 1941.

Even after the issuing of the 1942 Anglo-Ethiopian Agreement, which was supposed to recognize a fully free and independent Ethiopia, some in Britain wished to hold onto some valuable pieces of colonial real estate, whether it be Eritrea or even the Ogaden region in eastern Ethiopia.

There was some talk of actually incorporating both the former Italian Somaliland and Ogaden with British Somaliland to create a Somalian superstate that the Brits referred to as "Greater Somalia." As for Eritrea, there was a scheme afoot to chop off the lowlands of Eritrea and absorb them into British Sudan, which shared geographic and religious similarities with that particular part of Sudan.

Northern Sudan was predominantly Muslim in makeup, and so was this section of Eritrea. The rest of Eritrea had a large Christian population and was closely linked to Tigray (they also spoke the Tigrayan dialect of Tigrigna); the British intended to incorporate that territory back into the Ethiopian fold. All of these schemes would ultimately come to nothing. By the end of World War Two, the tired and weary British could not hold together the empire they already had, let alone add more to it by lopping off parts of Eritrea and Ogaden.

For many, the most logical solution to the Eritrean problem seemed to be its incorporation with Ethiopia, which was what Emperor Haile Selassie had desired in the first place. The United Nations—the successor of the League of Nations—ultimately weighed in on this matter, and in 1952, Eritrea was incorporated into Ethiopia. However, the local population, by and large, was not happy with this arrangement.

Their anger is understandable. Eritrea had long been severed from Ethiopia and had its own unique culture and way of life. From the strong Islamic inclinations to the many years of living under Italian influence, it makes sense why the Eritreans did not feel connected to Ethiopia proper any longer.

One also has to keep in mind the simmering hostilities between Eritreans and Ethiopians due to the aftermath of the war itself. The Eritreans greatly assisted the Italians. It is accurate to say that Ethiopian troops fought just as many Eritreans during the Second Italo-Ethiopian War as they did Italians.

As such, it is easy to understand why the Eritreans, who had lived so long under Italian influence and with many of them fighting and dying for Italian causes, might have come to feel as if they had just been placed under military occupation. They had infamously aided the Italians in their invasion and occupation of Ethiopia only to end up conquered by the Ethiopians themselves!

Interestingly (and perhaps not surprising), Italy was a strong supporter of Eritrean independence early on. It is scandalous to think that after all of the trouble Italy caused, postwar Italy would meddle in Ethiopian affairs, but it seems that Italian officials just could not help themselves. And even though Italy was denied direct control over its former colony, it would become a strong supporter of Eritrean independence.

Ethiopian historian Bahru Zewde has gone as far as to assert that the Italians used their strong ties in Latin America to influence certain outcomes as it pertains to the fate of Eritrea. Zewde cites a commission that was created by the UN in 1948. The commission was tasked with surveying the Eritrean problem and coming up with a solution. The commission was made up of five international representatives, and one of them was from Guatemala.

Bahru Zewde insists that the Guatemalan representative was in the back pocket of the Italians and sent to do Italy's bidding. If true, this would prove to be a powerful indication of indirect meddling on the part of the Italians. Nevertheless, only two members of the five (the Guatemalan representative included) recommended Eritrean independence. As a result, the UN, under the auspices of UN Resolution 390, officially authorized the repatriation of Eritrea back to Ethiopia.

Regardless of the results, at the end of the day, the Eritreans desired independence more than anything else. And they were willing to fight for it. They fought for it all throughout Selassie's long reign and even after he was deposed in the fall of 1974 by a communist coup. They continued their struggle under the banner of the EPLF (Eritrean People's Liberation Front).

It was not until the communist Ethiopian regime of Mengistu Hailemariam was toppled in 1991 by another political group of militants, the TPLF (Tigray People's Liberation Front), which had the help of the EPLF, that a deal was struck to grant Eritrea autonomy. This was just one of the many loose ends left untied because of the Second Italo-Ethiopian War.

An ongoing problem in Ethiopia that perhaps the Italians helped unleash (or at least exacerbate) was the issue of regional differences among Ethiopians. The early 2020s have seen increased strife between the Ethiopian federal government and other regional groups, especially in the Tigray and Oromo regions.

It is important to note that these two regional groups were ones the Italians specifically courted as potential collaborators. In their effort to divide and conquer Ethiopia, the Italians routinely exploited any regional differences to their own end. They offered bribes and promises of autonomy in exchange for making Emperor Haile Selassie's job of thwarting the Italian invasion more difficult.

And once the Italian occupation had begun in earnest, the power vacuum it created had an even stronger effect, not just on these two contentious regions but also on the average Ethiopian in general. As Ethiopian historian and scholar Bahru Zewde put it, "Peasant rebellions, rare phenomena before the Italo-Ethiopian war, became almost endemic after it." In many ways, it was as if the Italians had opened up a Pandora's box of animosity, and the aftermath made it very difficult for subsequent Ethiopian rulers to put those troubles back into the box.

# Conclusion: Keeping the Invaders at Bay

It could be said that much of human history has revolved around the bigger power picking on the smaller one, of the larger geopolitical power picking on the weaker geopolitical power. Ethiopia was invaded by a country with greater economic and military strength for practically no other reason than the invaders' desire to do so. Such things have played out in history since time began, and they are still ongoing today.

Although the topic is still highly debatable, one might even lump in the Russian invasion of Ukraine, which occurred in the early 2020s, as a part of this category as well. If the world lived by the philosophy of might makes right, in which big powers could roll over smaller powers simply because they could, human civilization would be brutal and bloody.

As much as the Italians wished to restore the Roman Empire, their actions and fascist philosophy threatened to send the world back to a darker time, one not too dissimilar to what the Romans themselves experienced a couple of thousand years ago. In many ways, the Romans were a fascist regime. Historians and Roman civilization buffs might recoil at such a notion, but in reality, almost any powerful ancient civilization had fascist tendencies.

These civilizations lived by the sword and ensured their own survival by foisting their military might on others. The often-lauded Pax Romana, or "Roman Peace," was only possible because the Romans had shut down all of their most immediate enemies and antagonists. The Roman

Republic faced threats from North Africa, particularly from what we now call Libya, with Carthage and its champion, Hannibal Barca.

It was not hard for Hannibal and other Carthaginian warlords to launch assaults across the Mediterranean and threaten the Roman civilization. It was also quite easy for renegade pirates to ambush Roman citizens who dared to sail the waters. Even Julius Caesar was once kidnapped by pirates! Shortly after Caesar's death, the Roman Republic transformed into an empire that conquered the entire Mediterranean world.

Under Roman military might, the entire Mediterranean became nothing more than a "Roman lake." There would be no more incursions from North Africa and no more pirates threatening Roman citizens, not because some great peaceful understanding was made between civilizations but because the Romans had stepped on all of their neighbors' necks, making sure that no one was able to rise up to threaten them.

The Romans perhaps can be forgiven for much of their aggression since warfare was the primary means of settling disputes back in antiquity. However, the Italians' brand of fascism in the 1930s came at a time when world powers were thinking very carefully of alternative ways to handle international disputes. The world had just survived the First World War and had seen how arbitrary military alliances could lead to major warfare.

After that devasting flare-up, the leaders of the world came to realize that some sort of collective body to handle disputes needed to be established to prevent such a thing from ever happening again. If the world could lurch to a devastating world war over one lone incident (of course, other issues were at play, but the assassination attempt is seen as the trigger), what was to prevent such a thing from occurring over and over again?

And if the world blew up into a world war every time something bad happened, there might not be much of a world left. This worried line of thinking led the more mature and forward-thinking leaders on the world stage to forge the League of Nations. The League has since been lambasted as a colossal failure because it failed to prevent things like the Italian invasion of Ethiopia. But in reality, the League of Nations was a valuable institution.

Even though it failed to prevent the invasion, it still provided Ethiopia with a platform to continue to demand that the world hold fascist aggression accountable. Without the League of Nations and the establishment of a rudimentary form of international rules and standards, there would have been nowhere for the exiled leader Haile Selassie to turn. The League of Nations provided a glimmer of hope to the Ethiopian government-in-exile.

And despite all of the League of Nations' failures and inaction, it provided the framework for what would become the United Nations. Neither the League of Nations nor the United Nations are perfect, and both may not have always lived up to their charter, but they are a start. And one can only hope that if virulent fascists and aggressors ever significantly threaten the norms of international law and procedure, the United Nations and other international bodies will help us begin the work of keeping the invaders at bay.

Here's another book by Captivating History that you might like

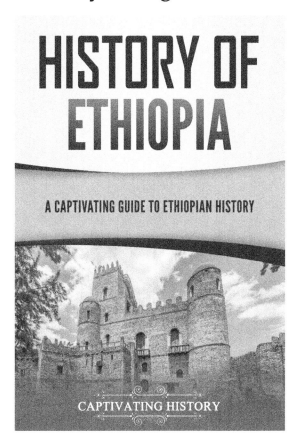

# Free Bonus from Captivating History (Available for a Limited time)

Hi History Lovers!

Now you have a chance to join our exclusive history list so you can get your first history ebook for free as well as discounts and a potential to get more history books for free! Simply visit the link below to join.

Captivatinghistory.com/ebook

Also, make sure to follow us on Facebook, Twitter and Youtube by searching for Captivating History.

# Appendix A: Further Reading and Reference

Campbell, Ian. *The Addis Ababa Massacre: Italy's National Shame*. 2017.

Dugan, James. *Days of Emperor and Clown: The Italo-Ethiopian War, 1935-1936*. 1973.

Gooch, John. *Mussolini's War: Fascist Italy from Triumph to Collapse: 1936-1943*. 2020.

Sbacchi, Alberto. *Ethiopia under Mussolini: Fascism and the Colonial Experience*. 1985.

Zewde, Bahru. *A History of Modern Ethiopia: 1855-1991*. 2001.

Printed in Great Britain
by Amazon

46395506R00050